Matching the Hatch

Stillwater, River and Stream
by
Pat O'Reilly

Macro photography by
Melvin Grey

SWAN·HILL
PRESS

Copyright © 1997 Pat O'Reilly

First published in the UK in 1997
by Swan Hill Press, an imprint of Airlife Publishing Ltd

British Library Cataloguing-in-Publication Data
A catalogue record for this book
is available from the British Library

ISBN 1 85310 822 7

Typeset by Phoenix Typesetting, Ilkley, West Yorkshire
Printed in Hong Kong

Swan Hill Press

an imprint of Airlife Publishing Ltd
101 Longden Road, Shrewsbury, SY3 9EB, England.

Contents

Preface 5

Part I - Matching the Form
1. From the Trout's Point of View 8
2. Order from Chaos 20
3. The Magnificent Seven 46

Part II - Matching The Munch
4. Spring 56
5. Summer 112
6. Autumn and Winter 180
7. All the Year Round 192

Part III - The DIY Entomologist
8. Further Investigations 210

Appendix I: Identity Parade 214
Appendix II: The Deadly Dozen 220
Further Reading 221

Index 223
  General Index 223
  Index of Common Names 223
  Index of Scientific Names 224

Acknowledgements

Gathering the information for this book has been great fun, and all the more so because of the tremendous support so generously given by friends in the game-fishing world. Many of the top experts on flyfishing and fly tying kindly agreed to tie flies for this book; in most instances the flies illustrated are their own designs which have now become standard patterns used throughout the world. Their tying skills greatly surpass my own, and so I am deeply indebted to Jon Beer, Brian Clarke, Alice Conba, Donald Downs, Peter Gathercole, Malcolm Greenhalgh, Melvin Grey, Derek Hoskin, Nigel Jackson, Charles Jardine, Steffan Jones, Peter Masters, Guy Mawle, Peter O'Reilly, Steve Parton, Neil Patterson, John Riegen, Andrew Ryan, Bernard Venables, Conrad Voss Bark, Mike Weaver, John Wilshaw and Davy Wotton. Peter Masters, of Masters Quality Fly Tying Materials, also tied several of the traditional patterns illustrated in this book.

Thanks are also due to the many friends who invited Melvin and me onto their fisheries to collect insects (and on occasions gave up their own time to join in the search), including Stuart Crabb, Neil Elbourne, Paul Knight, Patrick Lloyd, Stuart and Fiona McTeare, John O'Gorman, Joe O'Neil, Peter O'Reilly, Doug and Jacky Quigley, John Riegen and Andrew Ryan.

Finally, to Melvin Grey, the most dedicated and patient wildlife photographer I have ever met, a heartfelt thank you for working with me on this project and for making the experience such an enjoyable one.

Preface

Matching the hatch by using an artificial fly sufficiently similar to the creatures on which the trout are feeding can greatly increase your chances of success. That is not to suggest it is every day on every river and lake that the trout feed in a selective way; sometimes all that the fish are looking for is food, and then just about any fly fished in a realistic way will do the job. But when trout are being selective they may lock on to one particular type of insect – perhaps even to just one stage in the life-cycle of that insect – and then Lady Luck smiles upon the angler who uses the right fly, fishes it in the right place and makes it behave like the natural insect.

Call in at the tackle shop or look through a mail-order catalogue and you are faced with a bewildering array of artificial flies. How are you to choose from the many hundreds of fly patterns and sizes? Many people never progress beyond a 'lucky dip' strategy, wasting valuable fishing time switching between one concoction and another in an attempt to find something a finicky trout might find acceptable. The main purpose of this book is to help you choose suitable flies and to suggest how you can fish them in a way that will catch fish – to rely less on luck and more on judgement. And most importantly, it will guide you in choosing from a few very effective flies. If you buy your flies, try the 'Magnificent Seven' recommended in Part I – yes, seven flies really will cover almost all of your needs. If you tie your own flies, copy the 'Deadly Dozen' in Appendix II; these superflies were devised by some of the best flyfishers in the world.

What is in a name

Not content with plain English names such as mayfly, midge and dragonfly, entomologists (people who study insects) use Latin and Greek. The advantage is that scientists all over the world can share their findings with confidence that they are all talking about the same insect. But from an angler's point of view, the scientific names often act as a barrier to learning about the creatures on which trout feed. Take heart: flyfishers do not need Latin and Greek. If the first angler to see a mayfly hatching had decided to call it 'cucumber', we would now be using artificial cucumbers to catch trout in springtime.

In this book the anglers' common names for the natural insects are used, but for those who want to take the study of angling entomology further the scientific names have been included, too.

How to use this book

Learning anything new takes time, and for most of us fishing time in particular is in short supply. So, if matching the hatch is completely new to you, turn to Part I of this book and get results right from day one. This first section is all about getting the general form of your flies more or less right. Often this is all you need do, and the 'Magnificent Seven' recommended in Part I will get you started.

Knowing what a particular fly looks like can be important, but you will also need to know where and when each type of food creature is likely to be available to the trout. Part II, the 'angling entomology' section, will help you choose artificial flies to suit the type of fishery you are going to visit at a particular time of the day and season of the year. Get to know what to look out for – the photographs of the most commonly encountered natural flies should make that easier – and then choose a suitable artificial fly and make it mimic the antics of the living (or dead!) fly the trout are feeding on. With the 'Deadly Dozen', a set of superflies from the experts, you will be able to match the hatch right through the season.

What, where, when and how

Books on angling entomology generally divide the creatures on which trout feed into groups based upon the scientific classification of species, beginning with the upwinged flies – the mayfly and its relatives – and then going on to discuss sedge flies and stoneflies before lumping everything else together as 'miscellaneous'. This is fine when the aim is to help readers identify particular species of flies, but probably not the best way to help someone who wants to learn how to match the hatch through the flyfishing year.

For most flyfishers the season begins in spring, and that is why Part II of this book begins with chapters on imitating those insects which normally feature on the trout's menu at that time of year. Summer, autumn and winter menus follow in sequence, with a further chapter on food creatures which are available throughout the year.

What next?

Once you begin studying the insects and other tiny creatures in, on and around the water, it is easy to get drawn into the subject much deeper than you need purely from an angling point of view. Part III is a brief introduction to the study of insects. It may not help you catch many more fish, but taking an interest in the natural life of rivers and lakes can turn a blank day into a truly enjoyable one.

Pat O'Reilly
West Wales, Autumn 1996

Part I
Matching the Form

A guide to choosing general representations of the most common groups of insects and other creatures on which trout feed.

Chapter 1
From the Trout's Point of View

What is it that alerts a trout to danger, and in particular to the danger inherent in an artificial fly? Is it really the strange appearance of this alien intruder in the trout's larder? Or is the problem more complex – a combination, perhaps, of the appearance, sound, smell and behaviour of the fly?

Experience suggests that, unfortunately, the answer often can be a combination of two or more of these factors. Our challenge as flyfishers is to try to work out which factors matter in a particular situation and then to deceive the fish into believing that all is well.

The place to start must be with the quarry, and in particular with the behaviour of trout. What do they eat? How do they distinguish between food and the many inedible morsels which drift past them? How do they see a fly? Do they see colours, and if so are they more sensitive to some colours than others? And what about sounds – can they hear an insect swimming or struggling in the water? These are just some of the many questions we would like answers to.

Fig. 2. Ireland's River Suir is a rich limestone river and its trout can be very selective in their feeding habits.

From the Trout's Point of View

Here are some observations:

- Young trout often try to eat things which are not food – they are far less discriminating than adult trout. Small fish only survive to become big fish if they eat food that is wholesome, and so only the more cautious small fry live to become ultra-wary adults.

- In waters where people pass by frequently, trout come to accept such activities as normal, whereas in wilderness fisheries the sight of people pointing or waving their arms will send fish scurrying for cover.

- Small fry need frequent snacks throughout the day; large trout like their food in large chunks and are less interested in tiny insects (although they do take a consuming interest in small fishes, including their own offspring).

- Where food is scarce the trout grow slowly, spending most of their day on the look-out for food. Any food will do! Where food is abundant, trout often have definite feeding times which coincide with the availability of a particular type of food creature; then they can become very selective feeders.

- Trout reared in stew-ponds never forget those high-protein food pellets that were thrown to them twice a day. Even so, any 'stockies' that survive their first few months of freedom do so by learning to discriminate between real insects and poor imitations.

- In fast-flowing waters, trout have little time to scrutinise food samples before the current whisks the meal away; there, even the most cautious of fish has to make snap decisions. Not so the trout of still or slow water, who has plenty of time to inspect a fly and may reject it if there is any cause for suspicion.

From this it is clear that tactics which work in one situation may not always be successful in others. We need to be able to work out what matters most. Is it the appearance of the fly, or its behaviour? Or is the appearance (perhaps suddenly) of an angler or their subsequent behaviour of far more significance? These are important issues and we will take them further in the rest of this Part.

Here is a question flyfishers often ask: Is there a logical way of choosing fly patterns when there is no hatch in progress? I think there is, and the matters discussed in the next few pages will help you to catch trout more consistently at such times.

What the trout sees

Sometimes a trout will rise to your dry fly only to shy away at the last moment. What gave the game away – something only visible to the trout at very short range? Scientific study has shown that trouts' eyes respond to much the same colour range as humans, but until a trout gets close to the surface its view of a floating fly is likely to be blurred. The implications for flyfishers are:

- It is the general form and colours, and perhaps also the sound vibrations, of an object in or on the water that attracts the trout's attention to the possibility of food. Only as it approaches closely can the trout ascertain whether it has in fact found a food morsel.

- If we can combine convincing behaviour of our fly with broadly realistic form and colours, then the trout may not bother to use its acute short-range vision before seizing it. This is a lot easier if a good hatch is in progress and the trout has already taken several natural flies without problems.

Silhouette or full-colour image?

A nymph swimming either below or at the same depth as a trout will be clearly visible, illuminated by light from the sky. But if the trout is resting on the river bed and the nymph is near the surface, what the trout sees will depend on the colour of the river bed, the weather and the time of day.

Fig. 3. Sub-surface fly seen against a bright sky.

If the sun is high and very little light is reflected from a murky river bed, the nymph will appear as a silhouette (Fig. 3). On the other hand, if the water is shallow with golden sand on the bed and with overhanging trees diffusing the daylight, a trout looking towards the surface is likely to see very clearly the colours of the nymph (Fig. 4). On balance, then, it seems sensible to use artificial nymphs which match in colour the natural insects.

Fig. 4. Sub-surface fly seen beside a shaded bank.

Sub-surface colour

Many fly-tying materials change colour when they get wet. For example, some tying threads and silks go a much darker shade when they are submerged.

Fig. 5 shows the same tying materials, the left-hand samples being dry and the right-hand wet. If you want to match the colour of an artificial fly to that of a swimming creature such as a nymph or larva, it is always worth wetting samples of the tying materials before making the comparison.

Signs of life

No matter how realistic a nymph may appear in terms of size, shape and colours, a trout is quite likely to overlook it if it shows no sign of life. Movement through the water is an important part of this, but it is only one part: real nymphs have legs that crawl and gills that breathe. Stiff, lifeless nymph bodies are rarely as effective as those with fibres that vibrate as the fly is moved along.

Fur and feather fibres have been used for centuries in the making of wet flies, and in recent years synthetic fibres have added to the range of textures and colours available for matching the appearance of insects. Stiff or semi-rigid plastics are useful for creating translucent, segmented bodies, but they need to be used in conjunction with flexible fibres to produce realistic simulations of living, breathing creatures.

Fig. 5. The same tying materials dry (left) and wet (right).

The window and the mirror

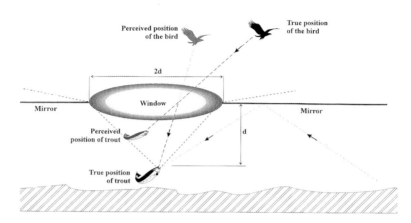

Fig. 6. How a trout views the outside world.

A bird flying over a calm lake and seeing a trout beneath the water may get a distorted view because of the bending of light rays by refraction at the surface. (You see this effect very clearly when you immerse the end of a stick in water: it appears to be 'broken' at the point where air and water meet.) Only when the bird is directly over-head will it see an undistorted picture; otherwise, the trout will appear to be further away horizontally but nearer to the surface than it really is. Similarly, the trout will see things that are above the water in a distorted way: the bird will appear to be more nearly overhead and at a slightly greater height than in reality it is.

As the bird moves away from the trout, the light rays are bent progressively more and more and an increasing proportion of the light is reflected from the surface rather than transmitted to the eyes of the trout. This means that the trout's picture of the outside world becomes more distorted as well as dimmer. Ultimately, if the trout looks towards the surface at an angle of 47° or more from the vertical, the only light it receives is that reflected from the underside of the surface; then, all that the trout can see is a reflected image of the bed of the lake. The surface acts like a huge mirror with a circular hole, or 'window', cut out directly above the trout's eyes. It is as if the window glass is clear over the middle region but tinted progressively darker towards the edges.

The fly in the mirror

Fig. 7. A dry fly leaving the mirror (the lower region of the picture) and entering the trout's window (the upper region of the picture).

In the mirror, any object that distorts the surface of the water may create a pattern of scattered light below the surface. This is because light incident on the meniscus – the curved water where surface tension supports the object – will penetrate below the surface. Because of this a fly line is far from invisible even when it is floating outside the trout's window, and so it seems sensible to use lightweight lines whenever possible simply because they are smaller in diameter and create less surface disturbance.

Even a tiny fly distorts the surface when it comes into contact with it. An upwinged dun floats with only its feet touching the water, and trout may come to recognise this characteristic pattern of light in the mirror. Unfortunately, many artificial flies float with their bodies touching the water and a hook point protruding below the surface. Note that both the hook point and its reflection in the mirror are visible – an obvious difference between the artificial fly and the real thing, and quite enough to tip off a cautious trout.

The distinctive outline of a swamped fly, with its wings and body trapped in the surface film, is also likely to be something a trout comes to associate with an easy meal. Some artificial spinners replicate this pattern very well, and probably as a result they catch more trout.

The fly in the window

Fig. 8. A dry fly just inside the trout's window.

If a dry fly drifts within the area of the window above a trout, then the trout is very likely to see it. Initially the shape will be fuzzy and distorted (Fig. 8), but it will become clearer as the fly comes closer to the centre of the window. Conversely, if the dry fly drifts past well beyond the edge of the trout's window it may go unnoticed. A simple calculation shows that the window diameter will always be near enough twice the depth at which the fish is swimming, and so this tells you how near your fly has to be to a trout if you want to catch it. (Of course, I am not saying the trout will always agree with the calculations; it may decide not to exert itself except for flies which come close to the centre of its window.)

A trout at the bottom of a lake 4 ft deep will have a window 8 ft in diameter, and it should be easy to use a leader long enough to keep the fly line well outside the trout's window. In water 6 ft deep a leader 12 ft long is barely enough to keep the end of the fly line out of the window.

Another implication of all this is that you will need to cast more accurately in shallow water if the trout is to see your fly at all. Not so when you are fishing deep water – unless, of course, the trout is swimming near the surface, as is common, for example, during a heavy fall of spinners.

Transmitted and reflected light

There is a complication when it comes to making nymphs: many of the natural insects are translucent, and so the colours that a trout sees are made up of both reflected light and transmitted light. For example, a nymph whose self-colour is a washed-out olive may appear to be brown when standing on bright pebbles and iridescent green when seen against a background of weeds. Ideally our artificial nymphs should have this characteristic. Translucent plastic fly-tying materials can be combined with fibres that wiggle as the fly moves through the water. Another approach is to tie nymphs in a range of body colours to suit different types of habitat.

Wings or no wings?

We know that in calm water the image of the river bed seen in the 'mirror' is broken up by six silvery points – the legs – if the insect is standing on the surface, but by a quite different pattern if it has collapsed into the surface. Ideally, then, our artificial flies should produce similar patterns, but very few come even close to doing so. So how closely should the shape of an artificial fly replicate that of the natural insect? And are wings really necessary?

In turbulent water the trout's picture of the fly is not very clear, and so such details as wings are rarely necessary when fishing a tumbling mountain stream. In calm water the situation is quite different. Initially the trout gets a hazy view of the fly as it leaves the mirror region and enters the window. The picture becomes clearer as the fly approaches the centre of the window and the trout rises to intercept it; the presence of wings can then make a difference.

Concealing the nylon

Floating nylon is a real give-away. Degreasing the leader tippet, and perhaps adding a weighted nymph a foot or so from the dry fly to pull the nylon below the surface, can help you to deceive wary trout in calm water.

Fig. 9. The upper nylon leader is floating on the surface. The lower leader is of the same diameter but it has been degreased so that it sinks just beneath the surface.

The trout's other senses

As well as a pair of ears concealed beneath the skin of its skull, a trout has vibration-sensitive organs along its lateral line and it can hear very well any sounds beneath the water. The question is: can a trout recognise the particular vibration patterns which are emitted by specific food creatures? If so, our artificial nymphs should ideally replicate these patterns. (Trout do seem to find nymphs that are tied with fibres which vibrate as the fly is drawn along more attractive than rigid-bodied nymphs.)

Background noise

On tumbling streams there is so much background noise under the water that the vibrations from an artificial nymph could only be discernible at close quarters. But on a quiet pool even a leaf falling can be enough to make a trout turn towards the possibility of a free meal; in these kinds of waters I suspect that nymphs whose body fibres move back and forth during the retrieve may emit vibrations which are detectable by the trout. For the same reason a sedge fly skittering in the surface at dusk is well represented by an artificial version tied with flexible fibres such as deer hair.

Taste and smell

Our own dietary preferences are based to a large extent upon the closely related senses of taste and smell (appearance and texture also concern us, of course), and so we might assume that trout also select from a menu of insects on the same basis. Personally, I doubt it. Trout do seem able to detect the scent of food – for example, an injured small fry releasing body juices into the water – but do they actually taste the individual tiny creatures that they swallow whole? Sometimes a freshly caught trout will have dozens of nymphs, larvae and pupae still alive inside its stomach; these insects have not been crushed and so they would not have released flavour juices. It seems reasonable, then, to assume that artificial flies are unlikely to be rejected because they do not have the right smell. Whether an artificial fly with the *wrong* smell would put off a trout is quite another matter: after peeling onions, for example, it might be wise to wash your hands before tying trout flies.

Some years ago an angler gathered together several species of insects and tasted them personally. Such dedication! He reported that they all tasted the same: ghastly. Of course, this in no way proves that all nymphs taste the same to a trout, but it is an assumption most of us are prepared to make without repeating the experiment.

The importance of texture

If the taste of an insect rarely matters to a trout, texture certainly does – and especially to grayling. With their relatively small mouths, grayling spend much of their time filtering food particles from the mud, and they soon learn to reject sticks and stones in favour of soft, squidgy nymphs and larvae. Artificial nymphs tied with copper wire may be fine for trout fishing, but a more pliable nymph is likely to work better when fishing for the Lady of the Stream.

When nymph fishing, detecting the take can be very difficult if a fish mouths the nymph well below the surface, and a lot of these takes must go undetected. Sometimes you see the leader dip down, but, by the time you strike, the fish has sensed that there is something not quite right with the meal and ejected it. Recently, Charles Jardine told me about some underwater observations which show that grayling hang on for quite some time to a soft artificial nymph but reject a solid one almost immediately – so quickly, in fact, that the angler may be quite unaware of having missed a take.

Frank Sawyer's woolly Killer Bug (Fig. 10) has attracted criticism because of its likeness to a maggot as used in coarse fishing. Sawyer's Avon holds good stocks of coarse fish in addition to its trout and grayling; however, this soft and squidgy grayling nymph works equally well on rivers which have no coarse fish. Is this because the fish hang on much longer than they would to a copper-wire nymph?

Fig. 10. Sawyer's Killer Bug (top) is much softer than the more wiry Pheasant Tail Nymph.

Inside the trout's head

It seems the brain-power of a young trout is barely enough to keep it alive – indeed, very few survive to maturity. Their simple computer program seems to be: 'If it's smaller than me and it moves, I'll eat it. If it's bigger than me and it moves, I'll beat it.'

Hunger and fear... what a childhood! But in time the young trout begins to recognise patterns – patterns of behaviour, of appearance and maybe of vibrations – which help it to discriminate between inert things drifting on the current and similarly sized objects (insects, for example) which move against the current. Eventually the trout may even come to recognise the particular patterns associated with individual types of food creatures. How carefully a trout scrutinises a fly and how preoccupied it is with one particular food type – these are the factors which determine how closely we need to imitate the real insects.

The hyper-cautious trout

On heavily fished waters the largest trout may be battle-scarred survivors of many campaigns, continually on the look-out for suspect flies. These hyper-cautious fish even reject a proportion of the natural flies that drift past, perhaps because of a crumpled wing or a missing tail. And when large, succulent mayflies first appear they are often viewed with suspicion and shunned for quite some time.

Fig. 11. 'Bridge' trout are well educated—many a flyfisher has had a go at these battle-scarred veterans.

Keep them in the dark

To catch an educated trout you will probably need a very close imitation of the natural creature it is feeding on at the time, and you will almost certainly need to cast skilfully from a place of concealment. As the evening light fades so your chances of success with these wily old stagers increase... but the odds may still be stacked against you.

So what general conclusions can we draw from all this? Here are some suggestions:

• In fast-flowing streams where food is scarce, wild trout are likely to accept any meal-sized offering. There, concealment and casting accuracy are more important than great delicacy of presentation.

• For wild trout in slow-flowing rivers where food is plentiful, it helps if you choose a reasonable general representation of the type of insect available at the time. During a heavy hatch or fall of flies, matching the hatch nearly always improves the prospect of success.

• To catch an educated trout you need a fly which closely imitates in appearance and behaviour the natural insect on which the fish is feeding. Concealment is also crucial, as are accuracy and delicacy of presentation. You may also need a bit of luck (or bad light).

Fig. 12. Matching the hatch (and a little luck) produced this fine brace of trout from Abbot's Barton on the River Itchen.

Chapter 2
Order from Chaos

Do you want to catch big trout? First the bad news: really big trout hardly ever eat flies – at least, not when they can find something more substantial. A 3 lb trout could lose weight chasing pin-sized insects, whereas he can live quite comfortably on the occasional 3 oz fish. And it does not appear to matter in the slightest to the trout if he eats his own kind!

And now the good news. In considering how you can improve your flyfishing results by 'matching the hatch', there is no need to exclude creatures which a trout will never see hatching – the flies that get blown in from the land, and the many other creepy-crawlies that can be imitated with artificial flies. In particular, imitations of various small fishes are often the most effective 'flies' if you want to tempt very big lake trout. Probably the most successful imitative flyfishers are those who, in a variety of situations throughout the year, are best able to 'match the munch'!

The main orders of insects

The flyfishers of the world could each have their own species of insect and there might still be plenty left over, because there are probably more than 15 million species of insects in the world. Only a small proportion of these are aquatic in origin, but many more are attracted to watery places and could quite conceivably be eaten by fish. Clearly, anglers have to be very selective.

Many successful flyfishers would not be able to identify more than about a dozen species of insects. They do not need to; this is not what matching the hatch is really about. But they do have a pretty good understanding of the basic appearance, habitat and behaviour of the most important *groups* of insects and of some of the more significant sub-divisions within these groups.

Scientists call the groups orders. The subdivisions are families, then genera and finally individual species. Very rarely do anglers need to identify insects right down to species level; more often it is general characteristics we need to copy and, not surprisingly, these are to be found at genus level.

The menu headings

Trout can be extremely catholic in their taste, giving almost anything a try; this is in sharp contrast to the selective feeding patterns we see occasionally. So, matching the hatch might involve copying creatures from any of the following categories:

Upwinged flies	Dragonflies and damselflies
Sedge flies	Beetles
Stoneflies	Small fishes
Flat-winged flies	Various other creepy-crawlies

Going through the change

As far as the insect groups are concerned, trout can eat them at various stages of their life-cycles. Maturing insects go through significant changes of form, either developing their wings gradually or pupating rather as a caterpillar does before it hatches into a butterfly. The upwinged flies, stoneflies and damselflies are examples of orders where the wings form gradually during a nymphal stage. In contrast, the larvae of most sedge flies and some flat-winged flies develop inside cases made from various types of debris. Once fully grown, the larva changes form and the adult fly develops rapidly inside a pupal shuck. The pupa then rises to the surface and a winged insect emerges and takes to the air.

Fig. 13. Without some knowledge of the creatures on which trout feed, how do you choose wisely from even this modest selection of artificial flies?

The upwinged flies (Ephemeroptera)

There are more than forty species of upwinged flies in the British Isles, although several of these are seen very rarely. They get their common name from the habit of holding their wings upright above the body when at rest. An upwinged fly has a broad head, a thorax in three sections each of which carries a pair of legs, and a long, ten-segment abdomen usually tapering towards the rear and terminating in either two or three long tails.

All upwinged flies go through four distinct phases: egg, nymph, dun and spinner. The first two phases are spent under water, while duns and spinners are the winged stages in the life-cycle.

The nymph

The nymphs, which have three tails, develop from tiny eggs and feed mainly on algae and rotting vegetation. As they grow, the nymphs shed their external skeleton many times, rather as crabs and lobsters do. After typically one year, the nymphs are ready to 'hatch' into winged insects. This they generally do either at the surface or by crawling out of the water. There are also a few species of upwinged flies which turn into the winged form while under water; in Britain we have just one, called the dusky yellowstreak.

Fig. 14. Nymphs come in many shapes and sizes.

Nymphs of the upwinged flies are usually categorised according to the way they have adapted to suit different types of habitat. The groups were defined by Oliver Kite, and are as follows.

- **Burrowers:** nymphs which live in tunnels beneath the mud, sand and gravel, venturing above the bed of the river or the lake only when ready to hatch. In the British Isles, the mayfly alone falls into this category; it has feathery gills arched over its body and these help keep a current of water flowing through the tunnel so that the nymph can obtain oxygen.

- **Silt crawlers:** a group of tiny nymphs which crawl upon the silty beds of rivers and lakes, feeding among the detritus. The Caënis nymphs are included in this group. These nymphs are covered in tiny hairs which collect a fine coating of silt debris, thus providing the nymph with camouflage – its only defence mechanism.

- **Stone clingers:** a third group of relatively inactive nymphs which spend most of their time clinging to the undersides of stones, where they feed by grazing on algae. The stone clingers are rarely seen swimming about; indeed, many come out only at night when the trout are less likely to find them. The nymph of the march brown is an example of a stone clinger, and its flattened shape and powerful legs help it to hold position in a strong current.

- **Moss creepers:** a very feeble-swimming group of nymphs, which feed among mosses on the river bed. The moderately flattened nymph of the blue-winged olive, which avoids predators by climbing under stones or into dense weed, belongs to this group.

- **Laboured swimmers:** a small group of slightly flattened nymphs which spend most of their time in the margins and can swim from place to place, but only slowly. The claret nymph is one of the laboured swimmers and is almost invisible when viewed against a background of the peaty margins of an upland lake.

- **Agile darters:** torpedo-shaped creatures of special interest to anglers because they swim rapidly from place to place in search of new feeding spots and are therefore available to trout even when there is no hatch of flies. The iron blue is one of the flies whose nymph can dart rapidly away from danger.

Emergers and duns

From the nymphal case a fly called a dun emerges. (The upwinged flies are unique in having this juvenile winged stage between nymph and mature adult.) The dun's wings are dull and fringed with tiny hairs, and its tails are much longer than those of the nymph from which it hatched. Once its wings have dried sufficiently, the dun takes off and heads for the cover of trees or bushes; there it rests until ready to shed one more skin in preparation for its final act of mating.

In damp weather it can take from several seconds to a minute or more for the dun to free itself from its nymphal case. Depending on the species, a proportion of duns fail to emerge fully and so remain trapped in the surface until they die – or until they are put out of their misery by a hungry trout.

Trout also feed on crippled flies. These are duns which, in escaping from their nymphal cases, damage their wings or get blown over onto their sides and fail to break free from the surface film. Few winged dry flies land upright on the surface every time they are cast, and the fact that trout readily accept them may, in part at least, be due to their similarity to crippled duns.

Duns usually darken quite noticeably soon after hatching, but it is mainly the newly hatched dun that a trout will come to recognise. When choosing fly-tying materials for matching the hatch, therefore, it is the colours of the newly emerged duns that we need to copy in order to produce the closest imitation.

Fig. 15. A newly emerged yellow may dun.

The egg-laying spinner
After anything from a few seconds in the case of the smallest upwinged flies to several days for some larger species, the dun splits its skin once more and out crawls the mature adult fly. Scientists call this an imago; anglers generally use the term spinner. The imago is a brighter fly than the dun. Gone are the hairy fringes and most of the colour from the wings, and the tails are noticeably longer than those of the dun. This stretching takes places within a few seconds of emergence, and then the external skeleton hardens and the insect is able to fly off in search of a mate.

Male spinners swarm, sometimes over or near the water but quite often some distance away. They rise and fall continually, waiting for a female to join them. When a female spinner flies into a column of male spinners she pairs up, and mating begins in the air. The paired flies often fall to the ground, where they separate and the female takes off and heads off back to the water.

Some spinners lay their eggs by alighting briefly on the surface and releasing a cluster of eggs; at this stage they are vulnerable, and many are taken by trout. The spinners of the *Baëtis* flies, a group which includes several important angling flies, crawl beneath the surface and attach their eggs to plants or sunken logs. (For example, large dark olive, pale watery and iron blue spinners all behave in this way.)

Fig. 16. Sparkling, transparent wings are characteristic of upwinged flies in their spinner stage.

The spent spinner

Once the spinner has released all of her eggs, she falls exhausted onto the water, flutters awhile until her wings become trapped in the surface film, and then drifts inert with her wings outstretched. Trout learn to recognise these easy pickings, and they rise leisurely to sip them from the surface.

Baëtis spinners that have crawled down below the surface to lay their eggs also end up as spent flies, but they approach the surface from the other direction and can become trapped just below it. It is usually easy to see when spent spinners are lying *on* the surface, but when trout are taking spinners trapped *below* the surface film they may appear to be feeding on nothing at all!

The males are usually smaller and often darker than the females. They also have larger eyes. A pair of claspers appended to the ninth segment of the abdomen are used to hold on to the female during mating.

Since many of the male spinners swarm and die well away from the water, it is the female that we most often want to copy, and in several species there is a marked colour difference between the sexes. The eyes and the claspers of the adult males are useful identifying features to help you to practise sex discrimination!

Fig. 17. This spinner has collapsed onto the surface after laying her eggs on the water.

The sedge flies (Tricoptera)

There are around 200 species of sedge or caddis flies in the British Isles, and they are found in all sorts of waters from chalk streams and lowland reservoirs to mountain torrents and moorland lakes. The adults look rather moth-like, and, like the moths, many species are nocturnal. There are, however, sedge flies which hatch by day, and many more whose emergence at dusk extends the evening rise, sometimes enticing to the surface some of the large trout for which other floating flies offer little or no attraction.

Sedge flies go through egg, larva, pupa and winged adult stages. This life-cycle is generally completed in one year, for most of which the insect is in its larval form. The pupal stage typically lasts a month or less and the adults can live from several days to a few weeks.

Caddis larvae

Sedge flies begin life as caterpillar-like larvae, commonly called caddis grubs. The majority of species live in portable cases which they build from materials gathered from the bed of the stream or lake. As a larva grows so it extends its home by cementing new material to the opening at the head end. Some species build with grit; others use plant stems, leaves, snail shells or sticks. The construction of a caddis case is a useful (but not infallible) guide to the species of adult which will later emerge from it.

Fig. 18. Sedge larvae build their cases in many varied forms.

Sedge Pupae

When the larva is fully grown, it secures its case to a weed stem or a stone and seals the ends of the case. The insect becomes a pupa, with a thin, transparent covering over the body but with at least the front two pairs of legs separated from the main chamber. Inside the pupal case the miracle of metamorphosis takes place over a period of several days to a few weeks. The pupa appears to change colour, often turning from grey or green to brown or orange; this is because the wings are forming, and many sedge flies have brownish wings. When the adult is fully developed inside the pupal shuck, the insect bites its way out of the end of the larval case and uses its free legs to swim up to the surface. Some species hatch at the surface; others paddle towards the shore and climb up emergent vegetation.

Those sedge pupae that hatch by day are extremely vulnerable during their journey to the surface and while paddling in the surface film; imitations of various types of sedge pupae are therefore of great value to flyfishers.

When sedges hatch in the evening, they are of interest to sea trout. As early in the year as mid-June, sea trout sometimes begin feeding on emerging sedges; at such times, a sedge pupa imitation can be an effective means of catching these enigmatic fish.

Fig. 19. The pupae of many summer sedge flies become adults in the late afternoon and evening, skittering on the surface and sometimes attracting the attention of trout which would not rise to lesser morsels.

Winged adult sedge flies

Sedge flies get their scientific name Tricoptera, meaning hairy wings, because the wings are indeed covered with hairs. This feature readily distinguishes them from some superficially similar moths whose wings are covered in minute scales which flake off into a fine powder when touched. Sedge flies have two pairs of wings which, when the insect is at rest, are held along the body in the form of a ridge tent. The adult sedge fly has a thorax in three sections, each carrying a pair of legs, a nine-section abdomen and no tails. Another characteristic of flies of this order is the long antennae – in many species more than double the body length.

Some types of daytime-flying sedges congregate just above the surface. Among these clouds of insects it seems there are always one or two with poor co-ordination, and occasional collisions occur. Although trout rarely leap at the clouds of flying sedges, a head-on collision often brings a fish up to deal with the casualties.

Nocturnal sedges are generally bigger than their diurnal relatives, and they do not tend to swarm; however, when they return to lay their eggs on moonlit nights a trout will sometimes surge upwards, turning at the last moment as it spots the insect which disturbed the surface and caused a momentary splash of light in the mirror. The result is a splashy, swirling rise which swamps the fly even if the trout does not take it at the first attempt. A buoyant artificial fly – the colour is rarely important – can give great sport at midnight and beyond.

Fig. 20. Adult sedge fly. Note the tiny hairs on the wings.

The Stoneflies (Plecoptera)

While on chalk streams and rich limestone rivers and lakes the stone-flies are less important than the upwings and the sedges, on most spate rivers, lochs and upland streams the stoneflies are a vital source of trout food, particularly in spring and autumn. Flies of this order, which contains around thirty species in the British Isles, are known as the Plecoptera, or hard-winged flies.

The smaller stoneflies complete their life-cycle in one year, but some of the larger ones take at least two years and possibly three. A stonefly has a life-cycle similar to that of an upwinged fly except that there is only one winged adult stage.

Nymphs

The nymphs generally prefer fast-flowing stony streams and the shores of large lakes where wave action oxygenates the water and exposes gravel or stones. One or two of the smaller stonefly species are to be found in weedy streams but rarely in great numbers. The nymphs grow through several stages, called instars, each time shedding their skins.

Stonefly nymphs have two tails, and so they can be immediately distinguished from the three-tailed nymphs of the upwinged flies.

Fig. 21. A large stonefly nymph.

Adult stoneflies

Stoneflies generally hatch by crawling out onto stones in shallow water or up emerging vegetation. This method of hatching is not an easy antic to mimic without the artificial fly getting snagged on the bottom. The adult stoneflies are therefore of greatest importance to flyfishers.

Most of the stoneflies of early and late season are dark brown or grey, often with a yellowish tinge to the underside of the body. These are the flies that hatch when upwinged insects are not so plentiful, and on spate rivers they can constitute a significant proportion of the spring and autumn fare for trout and grayling. Apart from the dark stoneflies, there are also two very common summer species with yellow wings and a few others with mottled brown wings.

Stoneflies have four wings of more or less equal length. The males of many of the larger species have very short wings and can only hop or crawl around, and so the females have to do the courting. After mating, the female stonefly lays her eggs, either by dropping them onto the water or by dipping down to the surface. For species where the wings continue beating during egg-laying, artificial stoneflies can be tied without clearly defined wings.

After laying their eggs, spent stoneflies often struggle and sink below the surface film; perhaps that is why some of the most effective imitations are tied in a spidery wet-fly style.

Fig. 22. A large stonefly.

Flat-winged flies (Diptera)

This is a very varied order of insects, with many thousands of species occurring in the British Isles. Flies of this order have one pair of wings – hence the name Diptera, meaning two wings. Many of these insects are very tiny, and although some of the most important (to anglers) are not truly aquatic they congregate near water and can be blown onto the surface, where trout are ready to welcome them.

This diverse grouping includes the daddy-long-legs, mosquitoes and bluebottles. The chironomids (non-biting midges) are Diptera, too, and they are a major source of food for trout in most stillwaters and in many rivers and streams.

All of the Diptera order go through egg, larva, pupa and adult stages, and there is tremendous variation between families of flies in this order. They vary greatly not only in size, shape, colour and preferred habitat but also in behaviour. It is not reasonable, therefore, to recommend a general representation to match the flat-winged flies, and so in Part II each important family group is discussed separately.

For the present, we will consider just one of these families, the chironomid 'buzzer' midges, and use this group of insects to discuss the fascinating life-cycles of insects in this order.

Fig. 23. The large cranefly, one of the biggest insects in the Diptera order, is seen here with a chironomid midge and a reed smut, its smaller relatives.

Midge larva

The worm-like larvae of chironomid midges live in decaying matter on the bed of a lake or in the slack water margins of a river. Most species live in tunnels constructed from silt and sand and attached to vegetable matter, stones or simply to one another. On silty lakes, the larval cases pile up in their millions and rather resemble All Bran.

The larvae themselves come in many colours ranging from olive and brown through red and purple to black. From the red larva comes the popular name bloodworm. A few midge larvae are free-swimming and travel erratically with a violent lashing movement which is not easily replicated with an artificial fly.

In rivers, grayling in particular feed extensively on midge larvae, sifting them from the silt. Imitations of the midge larva are sometimes useful, both on rivers and on stillwaters, and so in Part II a very effective bloodworm imitation is described.

In lakes and reservoirs, chironomid larvae inhabit water up to 20 ft deep. Quite often the best hatches come from the deeper areas, particularly on warm summer evenings.

The transformation from larva to pupa takes several days, during which time a 'bloodwormy buzzer pupa' – a mid-change stage – may also be worth imitating, as Steve Parton pointed out to me recently. Such a pattern is included in Part II.

Fig. 24. Chironomid midge larvae, or bloodworms, some of which have left their tube-like cases (also shown).

Midge pupa

When a bloodworm pupates, the winged adult forms rapidly inside a pupal case. Sprigs of fine pale filaments, looking rather like ears, develop on each side of the head when the pupa is ready to leave its larval mud tube. Usually within a day or two the midge pupa has a relatively large, ginger-coloured 'head' – in fact this section of the pupa also contains the developing thorax and wings of the insect – and the seven-segment thorax changes to the colour of the adult insect. A bunch of pale filaments appears at the tail end of the pupa; these, and the breathing gills at the head, are features which can be copied when tying artificial buzzer pupae.

When fully formed, the pupae rise up towards the surface. They are able to swim, but only weakly. This they do by folding the abdomen round under the head and then kicking it out straight. Each kick typically allows the pupa to shift position by an inch or two. The direction of this movement appears somewhat random, but by a series of contractions and kicks they are able to move along as well as up and down in the water.

Once the pupa reaches the surface, it may rest in the film for a few seconds or for several minutes depending, probably, on water conditions. Eventually the pupal case splits open and the adult fly emerges. During the ascent and while breaking through the surface film many of these insects become trout food, and the resulting rise can be quite spectacular when conditions are favourable.

Fig. 25. A buzzer pupa at the point of 'hatching' into an adult fly.

Adult midge

Once out of their pupal shucks, adult midges leave the surface as if equipped with ejector seats. It is therefore the egg-laying females and any wind-borne casualties that feature on the trout's menu. Most species are believed to produce two or more generations per year, so there are buzzers to be seen (and heard) throughout the season.

The wings of the midge are considerably shorter than the body, and this feature should be copied when tying imitations of the adult midge. The main difference between males and females is that females have fatter abdomens and only the males have their antennae decorated with feathery plumes. As with most insects, the males are somewhat smaller than their mates.

In early spring, medium-sized black midges such as the blae and black and the duck fly are often the first to appear in large numbers. Olive, ginger and brown midges are also common in spring, and these flies usually reappear later in the year.

Adult midges can be important sources of food on stillwaters in the evenings, when trout rise to the females which return to lay their eggs. On calm evenings a dry fly can be successful, but in choppy water the flies soon get swamped and so a wet fly just beneath the surface is often more effective. Imitations which are the right size and general colour get good results, and so matching to species level is generally considered quite unnecessary.

Fig. 26. This chironomid midge emerged in early spring, but similar hatches continue right through the summer months.

Aquatic beetles

There are a great many species of aquatic beetles, some of which spend their time paddling around on the surface while others, notably the various species of diving beetles, live under the water and come up to the surface only occasionally to replenish their air supply.

Beetles have an egg-larva-pupa-adult life-cycle, and the change between larva and adult is quite startling. The larvae usually leave the water to pupate either in wet soil or among the roots of marginal plants. Upon hatching into their adult form, the beetles return to the water, occasionally venturing well away from the margins and so putting themselves on the trout's menu.

Fig. 27. The larva of the great diving beetle, *Dytiscus marginalis*, can attain a length of 50 mm. This conveniently hook-shaped creature lives among dense vegetation.

Adult beetles

Among the aquatic beetles commonly found in the margins of lakes and slow-flowing rivers are the great diving beetles (*Dytiscus* species), whirligig beetles (*Gyrinus* species) and silver water beetles (*Hydrophilus* species). Silver water beetles can grow to well over 50 mm in length. Seldom are diving beetles found in open water in sufficient numbers for trout to become preoccupied with them as a food source; indeed, rarely are these creatures found during trout autopsies, and so efforts to devise matching imitations of aquatic beetles are probably of limited value. Beetle larvae are sometimes taken by trout, however, and an imitation may be worth developing.

Fig. 28. The adult great diving beetle is a fiersome beast, quite capable of holding its own . . . or yours if you try to handle it!

Terrestrial beetles

In upland regions, terrestrial beetles of various sorts contribute significantly to the food supply of trout in the summer and autumn months. In most instances these are insects whose larval and pupal stages are terrestrial, and so it is the adult beetle which offers most opportunity for the flyfisher. The coch-y-bonddu, a beetle which hatches in summer is discussed in Part II, but there are many others worth looking out for.

Because food for trout is always in short supply at high altitudes, matching the hatch is only likely to make a real difference if you are fishing waters which are subject to heavy angling pressure and the trout have been educated into scrutinising each morsel. In most places the fish are so anxious to grab what is available before it gets away (or before a neighbour takes it) that they throw themselves at beetles with complete abandon. At best, all you need is a beetle-shaped fly of about the right size and colour.

There are numerous species of black beetles, including the common ground beetles which seem to be attracted to water but have no sense of danger, the staph or rove beetles, and the sailor beetle. The sailor beetle, *Cantharis rustica*, is very similar to the soldier beetle (page 172), but instead of the familiar orange-brown wing case it wears a dark blue uniform.

Drowning beetles can be imitated by one of the many black spider wet flies or by a 'dry' pattern fished awash in the surface film.

Fig. 29. The sailor beetle is plentiful in many upland regions.

The dragonflies (Odonata)

The brilliantly colourful dragonflies (of the sub-order Anisoptera) are among the most attractive of aquatic insects. They inhabit most lowland stillwaters and the slower-flowing reaches of rivers.

Fig. 30. Dragonfly nymphs (this is a *Sympetrum* species) are slow crawlers, but by ejecting water from the rear they are able to pounce on their prey or to escape a lunging predator.

Dragonflies go through egg, nymph and adult stages. The nymphs, which take two or more years to reach maturity, are most commonly found either in the muddy beds of quiet backwaters or among dense marginal vegetation. They feed on insects, tadpoles and fish fry. Most dragonfly nymphs are brownish except just after moulting a skin, when the newly emerged nymph is pale green or olive.

In summer, dragonfly nymphs hatch by crawling up waterside plants and resting above the surface until their nymphal skins split and the adult insects emerge.

Trout in lakes can sometimes be seen leaping at paired dragonflies as the female repeatedly dips her abdomen into the water to lay eggs close against the bank. Occasionally as it darts across a lake, skimming the surface in search of hatching flies, a dragonfly will suffer a direct hit from a well-aimed missile attack in the form of an acrobatic brown trout. From the angler's viewpoint, however, the main interest in these insects is their spectacular aerobatics displays: by moving each of their four wings independently, dragonflies are able to fly sideways and even backwards.

Fig. 31. The common red darter dragonfly (*Sympetrum striolatum*) is seen on many stillwaters during warm, sunny days.

Adult dragonflies

Dragonflies and the closely related damselflies are sometimes confused – both belong to the order Odonata. The front and rear wings of dragonflies are of different sizes, the rear wings being broader and slightly shorter than the forewings, and at rest the wings are directed away from the body. (Damselflies have equal wings, held aligned with or only at an acute angle to the body.)

The 'hawker' types of dragonflies rely on ambush to surprise their prey. They will hover above the water until a smaller insect approaches; then they dive on their dinner, holding their hairy legs in the shape of a basket, into which the prey insect is swept.

Fig. 32. *Aeschna cyanea*, the southern hawker, is frequently seen on canals and stillwaters.

The 'darter' and 'chaser' dragonflies use speed and manoeuvrability to secure their meals; they can fly at more than 10 miles per hour.

Fig. 33. This broad-bodied chaser (*Libellula depressa*) is fairly common in the south of England and in Wales.

The damselflies

Damselflies (of the sub-order Zygoptera) are more delicate than their larger relatives the dragonflies. The adults and, most particularly, their nymphs are important sources of food for trout.

Damselflies have a life-cycle very similar to that of the dragonflies. The egg hatches into a nymph which grows slowly through the winter months and then more rapidly in spring and early summer. The adults emerge in summer and some species are on the wing until October.

Fig. 34. A damsel nymph. This *Calopteryx* species occurs in the slower stretches of rivers and streams.

Damsel nymphs

Damselfly nymphs are readily available to trout. They populate lakes and slow-flowing rivers wherever the water is shallow enough for light to penetrate the bed and allow mosses and submerged weeds to grow. As the damsel nymphs approach maturity, usually over a one-year cycle, they migrate towards the shallower margins. Trout feast well on damsel nymphs at this critical stage in their life-cycle.

Early in the morning, damsel nymphs climb up emergent weed stems. As the air warms up, they split their shucks and out crawl the adult flies. The wings stretch to their full size over a period of a few minutes as blood is pumped into the veins, and within an hour or so the wings harden and the adult insects are ready to take flight.

Fig. 35. The banded demoiselle *(Calopteryx splendens)*. The female, seen here on the right, does not have the dark banding on its wings.

Damsel hatching sequence

Damselflies offer the angler a unique opportunity to observe the nymph-to-adult hatching process in slow motion. This sequence of pictures was taken over a period of fifty minutes.

Fig. 36. The nymph has just crawled up a plant stem and selected its hatching site above the water.

Fig. 37. The damselfly has crawled clear of its nymphal shuck.

Fig. 38. The common blue damsel (*Enalagma cyathigerum*) is now ready for her maiden flight.

Water bugs (Hemiptera)

This order includes several creatures which live in such dense vegetation that they must rarely be seen by trout. A few examples are illustrated here, while the more important ones from an angling viewpoint are covered in Part II.

Surface water bugs

The greater waterboatman lies upside down in the surface film and dives to seize its prey, while the pond skater and many similar water bugs spend most of their time on the surface. There is no doubt that trout will feed opportunistically on surface bugs that die and get blown into a lea shore. A black or brown spidery dry fly cast into the margins in the early morning can surprise a grave-robbing trout.

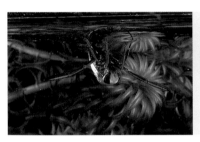

Fig. 39. The greater waterboatman or backswimmer (*Notonecta* species) can grow to 20 mm long.

Fig. 40. A pond skater. These rapidly darting surface dwellers (*Gerris* species), typically growing to between 10 and 15 mm in length, also inhabit the margins of slow rivers.

Fig. 41. The water measurer (*Hydrometra* species) is normally seen walking slowly across the surface, but it can also walk down plant stems under the water.

Sub-surface water bugs

The common water bug (*Aphelocheirus montandoni*) spends its life scuttling around the beds of weedy chalk streams. Similar species are also found in spate rivers, where they tend to concentrate in those sections where moss-covered boulders provide them with respite from the strong current. When necessary, these disc-like creatures can swim surprisingly quickly.

Fig. 42. The common water bug, a disc-like insect found in most chalk streams, is also common in some spate rivers. This sample came from the River Monnow.

Stick insects (*Ranatra* species) have long breathing tubes by which they hang from the surface until a food creature approaches. They move very slowly and are superbly camouflaged among the weed stems. Their front legs are adapted, like those of the preying mantis, for seizing their prey. A similar creature, but with a fatter body, is the water scorpion, *Nepa cinerea*, which can grow to a length of 30 mm.

Fig. 43. This stick insect, from Rhydlewis Trout Lake in West Wales, is 60 mm long.

Trout and water bugs

Most of the sub-surface water bugs live among dense marginal weeds, and autopsies on trout show that only occasionally do they eat these kinds of insects. There is, however, one exception: trout do sometimes feed selectively on lesser water boatmen (*Corixa* species). For the still-water anglers, the *Corixa* is by far the most important of the water bugs, and so this insect and its matching artificial are covered in Part II (pages 194 and 195).

Small fishes

A really disappointing discovery, as far as flyfishers are concerned, is that large trout do not live on flies. They may, occasionally, be tempted into taking a snack by a passing nymph or water bug, but by and large they prefer to eat large meals without exerting themselves unduly – it is the only way to grow big in the underwater world. So the angler who uses fish-like lures is probably coming as close to matching the munch as it is currently possible to do.

Prey species

In still or slow water, there are a great many species of game and coarse fish which might be expected to feature on the trout's menu at various times of year. One- and two-year old roach, dace, perch and gudgeon are commonly found in the stomachs of trout caught during the summer months, while in autumn the small fry which hatched just a few months earlier are greatly thinned down by fry-guzzling trout which hunt them in the shallow margins.

In lowland rivers, trout and other predatory fish and birds are kept well fed by the shoals of sticklebacks which patrol the shallows. Imitations of these, and some other fishes on which trout frequently feed in a selective way, are included in Part II.

Finally, it is worth mentioning that large trout are in no way averse to eating trout and salmon parr.

Fig. 44. A shoal of sticklebacks must present a mouthwatering prospect for a hungry trout.

Chapter 3
The Magnificent Seven

Surely one of the worst nightmares for a flyfisher would be to discover a fly pattern that is all things to all trout: a fly which any trout would find irresistible at all times. That would be the end of civilised flyfishing as we know it. There have, of course, been instances where a new fly pattern has done exceptionally well – so well, in some cases, that nervous proprietors have banned it from their fisheries. The Alexandra – an attractor pattern rather than an imitator, admittedly – was one such, and who knows, without this dubious distinction would it be so well known today?

A 'one fly' strategy works reasonably well with recently stocked hatchery-reared trout. It is also fairly successful in upland wilderness fisheries where the trout are only too pleased to see any insect drop in for lunch. But for wild trout on lowland fisheries where food is plentiful, the idea of trout accepting one artificial fly at all times remains just a nightmare (thank goodness) and when trout are feeding selectively the 'one fly' approach fails more often than not.

7,000 flies . . . or just seven?

If one fly will not suffice, surely the newcomer to the sport of flyfishing does not have to gather and study a collection of the many thousands of fly patterns which have been devised over the years. Well, this I can say with complete confidence: some simplification is certainly possible. Instead of 7,000 flies, why not start with just seven?

The 'Magnificent Seven', as I call them, are general imitations. They will not enable you to catch every trout you see . . . but then, neither would 7,000 patterns. They do, however, cater for the vast majority of situations where a general imitation will do, and that means most places, most of the time. The Magnificent Seven cover the main categories of shapes and colours. You will need two sizes of some of them.

They are all patterns which you can buy in most good tackle shops, but basic tying ingredients are also listed for those who are already into fly tying.

Group 1: agile darting nymphs and stonefly nymphs

The torpedo-shaped agile darters, such as the nymphs of the *Baëtis* flies and the pond olives and lake olives, call for slim-bodied imitations. Ideally, it should be possible to tie versions of the fly in such a way that it can be fished near the bottom, near the surface, or in the surface film to represent an emerger.

Gold-ribbed Hare's Ear (GRHE) (Sizes 14 and 16)

The simple GRHE has spawned many variations; however, in the turbulent waters of a fast-flowing chalk stream or a tumbling spate river, the size of your artificial nymph, the depth at which you fish and the movement you impart to your nymph are far more important than any tying refinements you could make to this classic design.

The tail and body fibres are dark fur taken from the base of a hare's ear. The body is ribbed with flat gold tinsel, and to represent the legs of a nymph or the curled-up wings of an emerging dun a few long body fibres are picked out. The tying thread is yellow.

Fishing tip
The GRHE can be adapted for deep nymph fishing. Tied with a lead underbody, it will sink rapidly. Once the nymph comes alongside a trout, a lift of the rod tip will make it come alive – a tactic which often results in an 'induced take'.

Fig. 45. One of many versions of the GRHE, this plumped out emerger is from Bernard Venables (Mr Crabtree).

Group 2: dark duns and spinners, and stoneflies

On rivers and on stillwaters, many of the upwinged flies of spring and autumn have drab olive bodies at the dun stage and brownish bodies as spinners. At the same time, dark-bodied stoneflies are commonly encountered, although these are mainly restricted to flowing waters. A single pattern will often suffice as an imitation of these kinds of insects at times of the year when food is not so plentiful and the trout are less inclined to be fussy about their food. Indeed, on spate rivers where food is nearly always at a premium a general 'olive' pattern is likely to be a pretty good choice for daytime flyfishing throughout the season.

Greenwell's Glory (Sizes 12 and 16)

This fly dates back to 1854. It was developed by Cannon Greenwell and Mr James Wright for trout fishing on the Tweed, and it was originally dressed as a wet fly, without a tail.

Wet, dry and nymph versions of the Greenwell's Glory are used nowadays. The popular tying shown below is a dry fly and it works very well on lakes as well as rivers when olive-bodied flies are hatching. The Greenwell's will do good service as a general representation of most darkish winged insects. A furnace cock hackle or Greenwell hackle is used for the tail and also for the legs (unfortunately also called the 'hackle') of this fly. The body is waxed yellow tying thread with a gold wire rib, and the wings are starling.

Fig. 46. Greenwell's Glory.

Group 3: light duns and spinners

In the great majority of upwinged flies, the wings of spinners are transparent, sometimes with brown veining, and so a fly with an overall lighter appearance gives a better colour match than can be achieved with the Greenwell's Glory. There are also a number of pale duns – a group formerly referred to as the 'pale wateries', although nowadays this name is usually reserved for one particular species – and a pale-bodied fly is useful as a general representation of these upwinged flies also.

Tups Indispensable (sizes 14 and 16)

This fly dates back to 1900, when a Mr R S Austin first tied it. He, and after his death his daughter, kept the dressing a secret for many years and supplied flies to the secret recipe. The father of modern nymph fishing, G E M Skues, eventually named the fly when, in 1934, it was revealed that the body dubbing contained hair from the testicles of a ram (hence 'tup').

The true Tups Indispensable uses yellow tying thread, a tail of yellow-spangled light blue cock hackle; a body dubbed with a mixture of white 'tup' fur, lemon spaniel fur and yellow mohair; and a yellow-spangled, light blue cock hackle. The modern dressing uses substitutes for some of the materials which are harder to obtain, and crimson seal fur replaces the yellow mohair.

Fig. 47. Tups Indispensable.

Group 4: sedge flies and alders

Sedge flies are important throughout the season but most particularly during the evenings in summer and autumn. They vary in size from micro-sedges less than 5 mm in length to the great red sedges which can be more than 25 mm long. Many commonly occurring species are between 8 and 12 mm long and are best matched with an artificial tied on a size 14 hook; they are mainly silvery-fawn or grey-brown with brown or greeny-brown bodies. A general sedge imitation should, therefore, have these characteristics.

Silver Sedge (sizes 12 and 16)

This is another of those traditional dry flies which have stood the test of time. There are numerous tying versions. The Silver Sedge is a good imitation of the many small, light-coloured sedges of summer, but it also serves as an excellent general sedge pattern for river fishing. I have had some success using this as an autumn grayling fly, but it is particularly good when fishing for trout on rivers and streams. In the larger size it is a useful pattern for stillwaters, too.

Because this fly represents a sedge, it is tied without a tail. The body is palmered with a red cock hackle (a short-fibred hackle is required) and ribbed with flat silver tinsel. The wing is usually from a coot, but starling is a suitable alternative. The wing slips should be tied in to slope back over the body. The hackle is of deep red cock, and the fly is whip finished to create a small head.

Fig. 48. One of many versions of the Silver Sedge.

Group 5: damsel nymphs and fish fry

Damselflies are greatly outnumbered by damsel nymphs, and trout are the main cause of this. As the damsel nymphs migrate towards the shore to hatch, so the trout lie in ambush and start their day with a 'full works' breakfast. An artificial damsel nymph is therefore an essential start to any stillwater flyfisher's armoury. (And on many slow-flowing rivers it is probable that the value of damsel nymphs as a source of trout food is often greatly underestimated by anglers preoccupied with upwinged flies.)

Throughout the season, but most particularly as autumn replaces summer, fish fry feature in the diets of lake trout and of river trout. A damsel nymph imitation, moved through the water with a fish-like action, may be all you need to lure a fry-feeding trout.

Damsel Nymph (sizes 10 and 12 long shank)

Bead-eyed Damsels are now available from many tackle shops. The tying varies considerably, but a common feature is a brass bead fitted just behind the eye of the hook. The body is usually olive SLF, Antron or marabou fibres, and a bushy marabou 'tail' (to represent the three tracheal gills of the natural insect) adds to the illusion of life.

As this fly is being retrieved jerkily through the water, the weighty head rises and falls, causing the marabou tail to sweep up and down. The result is a very lifelike action indeed.

Fig. 49. Bead-eyed Damsel Nymph, tied by Steffan Jones.

Group 6: beetles, midges, gnats and black flies

Throughout the season, but particularly from July onwards, there are numerous dark insects and spiders to be seen near water. Many of these get blown in and are eaten by trout, and so a general representation of something dark and fairly substantial is an invaluable component of a basic kit of flies.

Coch-y-bonddu (sizes 14 and 18)

There is a terrestrial beetle whose Welsh name is coch-y-bonddu, meaning 'red with a black trunk', and in upland regions it appears in great numbers during the summer months. The artificial fly going by the same name is, not surprisingly, a traditional Welsh pattern. It is an effective imitation of other beetles, including aquatic beetles, and can be used whenever small, dark creatures fall in to the water.

Normally used as a wet fly fished just under the surface, the Coch-y-bonddu will, if lightly oiled, float quite well, and so it is a useful addition to your dry fly box, too.

The dressing is very simple, using black tying thread, a gold tinsel tag – this may possibly be intended to represent an air bubble which most aquatic beetles need to carry with them when they swim below the surface – a body of bronze peacock herl, and a coch-y-bonddu hackle (this is the name flydressers give to a red game hackle with a black centre stripe and black tips).

Fig. 50. Coch-y-bonddu.

Group 7: buzzer pupae

Chironomid midges are so important – on stillwaters and on slow-flowing rivers – that they really do deserve a fairly accurate imitation of the life-cycle stage of most importance: the pupa. Not only that, but it is often the case that when trout are feeding on buzzer pupae just about every other type of insect or its imitation is steadfastly ignored.

Buzzer pupae come in many colours, of which probably the most common is olive, and so this is the colour chosen for the pattern described below. This pattern will also do very nicely if you find trout taking other sub-surface Diptera pupae such as those of mosquitoes.

Olive Suspender Buzzer (sizes 14 and 16)

This idea for suspending nymphs in the surface film was originally devised in America, but John Goddard has adapted it very success-fully to imitations of hatching midge pupae.

The 'tail', representing breathing filaments, is a small tuft of white wool of floss silk, the body is olive seal fur or Antron ribbed with seven turns of fine silver wire, and the thorax is peacock herl. The clever bit is the head: this consists of a little ball of Ethafoam wrapped in nylon stocking mesh and tied in just behind the eye of the hook.

This fly really is unsinkable!

Fig. 51. Suspender buzzer.

Size keys

In the chapters which follow, approximate sizes of flies from the more important orders are indicated by means of sketches at the top of the page. The sizes shown are typical of the females.

Upwinged flies

In the case of upwinged flies, the males are around 15 per cent smaller than their mates. It is not uncommon, however, for individual upwinged flies of the same species to vary by almost a factor of two, and so size alone is not particularly useful as a means of identifying species.

Sedge flies

It is not particularly easy to distinguish at a glance between the males and females of this order. The males are often slightly smaller than the females. The size variation from one individual to another is not as great as with the upwinged flies, and a range of 10–15 per cent either side of the norm can be expected for most species.

Stoneflies

While the body of a male stonefly is only slightly shorter than that of the corresponding female, the wings are invariably much shorter, giving the male a much smaller appearance overall.

Flat-winged flies

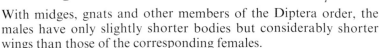

With midges, gnats and other members of the Diptera order, the males have only slightly shorter bodies but considerably shorter wings than those of the corresponding females.

Part II
Matching the Munch

A through-the-seasons guide to imitative flyfishing using the minimum of artificial fly patterns

Chapter 4
Spring

Early in the season the variety and numbers of aquatic insects are greatest. This is particularly noticeable during the daytime on lowland rivers and lakes, where trout rise far more readily to the surface fly at this time of year than they do in the heat of summer.

In March and April, feeding activity is concentrated around midday, but by mid-May the days have lengthened, the water has warmed up, and trout take flies and near-surface nymphs from early morning until late afternoon. After the middle of June there is usually a quiet period around midday on the richer lowland waters, and dry-fly fishing becomes more difficult as summer approaches.

Spring arrives later in the hills, and in terms of the daytime activity of insects and of trout it continues for longer, too. On mountain streams there may be no discernible 'siesta' until at least mid-July: there, trout rise whenever they get the chance of a snack. And on wooded hill streams, those bright summer days which send lowland trout scuttling for the cover of shaded lies are no problem: trout fishers enjoy the benefits of a built-in canopy which diffuses the light and allows insects and fish to go about their business as usual.

Fig. 53. April on a small stillwater.

The flies of spring

The upwinged flies of spring are generally larger than those which appear during the day in summer, and many are also darker than their fair-weather cousins. Several of the spring upwinged species cause selective rises, and so I have suggested specific imitations for these. With few exceptions spring duns are more important to flyfishers than are the spinners. This is because the spinners of most spring-hatching flies lay their eggs late in the day and trout either ignore them or do not even see them.

Most of the early-season sedge flies are fairly small with fawn or light brown wings. There are also one or two species of small stoneflies which can give good sport on cold spring days, particularly on fast-flowing rivers and streams.

Some important terrestrial insects appear early in the season. On upland fisheries they bring the first really significant rises, particularly in the windy conditions so typical of April and May. The daddy-long-legs flies of spring may not appear in such great hordes as their autumn relatives, but many of them are of aquatic origin and so they return to the water to lay their eggs. Trout love them!

Spring and autumn weather and water conditions can be similar. Not surprisingly, then, a few of the more common spring flies (or in some cases closely related species) reappear in the autumn. Also, few hatches are strictly confined to just two or three weeks: the mayfly of May and June is often seen in small numbers through to October!

Fig. 54. Spring trout fishing on a small stream.

Large dark olive

(Baëtis rhodani)

The large dark olive is an adaptable insect found both in small streams and in large rivers. It is equally at home in mildly acidic becks and alkaline chalk streams, but because it requires a strong current this fly is rarely encountered in lakes, and then only in the vicinity of inlet streams.

Despite its name the large dark olive is not such a big fly, but it is considerably bigger than any of the other *Baëtis* olives. This is the earliest of the upwinged flies to hatch in sufficient numbers to stir the interest of trout. In most rivers and streams on which this fly occurs you are likely to see its reappearance in late autumn.

Early in the season, large dark olives hatch from around midday until the middle of the afternoon; indeed, as far as dry-fly fishing on spring-fed rivers is concerned, this can be a very important grayling fly. On lowland spate rivers the large dark olives emerge in trickle hatches in early March and their numbers increase through the month. By late April the hatches are usually tailing off.

The autumn hatches are usually more sparse than those of spring-time, especially in the north of Britain, but from around the end of September right through the winter a few large dark olives are likely to trickle off whenever the weather is mild.

Fig. 55. The River Hodder has good hatches of large dark olives.

The large dark olive nymph

(a typical agile darter)

Fig. 56. Large dark olive nymph.

This nymph is an agile darter, and so it is worth imitating even when there is no hatch and the trout are not rising. At such times you will need a weighted nymph to search for trout feeding among the submerged weeds or around the stones on the river bed.

Like all other nymphs of the upwinged flies found in the British Isles, the large dark olive nymph has three tails. It is a strong swimmer, moving in spurts of jerky activity rarely lasting more than two seconds, during which time it travels a few inches. When ready to hatch, the nymph rises up to the surface and the dun emerges in open water.

Magnificent Seven: GRHE (see page 47), size 14. A closer imitation is unlikely to be necessary.

Fishing tip
Cast upstream of a nymphing trout and allow your weighted GRHE to sink. As the nymph comes alongside the trout (or where you suspect one is lying), lift the rod tip in a series of small jerks so that the nymph begins rising to the surface. Trout find these 'escaping' nymphs virtually irresistible. An induced take is usually indicated by the floating section of your leader dipping downwards.

The large dark olive dun

Fig. 57. Large dark olive dun (f).

The name 'olive' is used by anglers to describe several related species of upwinged flies, all of which retain just two tails in their adult stages. Most of these *baëtid* olives, including the large dark olive, have tiny hindwings which are difficult to see without an eyeglass.

On breezy days the duns often get blown onto their sides and a fair proportion fail to right themselves. Trapped in the surface film, they are easy prey for hungry trout; so, although the casting may be more difficult, windy spring days can often provide the best sport. A similar, but slightly smaller fly, *Baëtis atrebatinus*, extends the large dark olive hatch of springtime; its hatches are rarely dense, however, and for flyfishing purposes it can be treated as a large dark olive.

Magnificent Seven: Greenwell's Glory, size 14.

Fig. 58. The male dun of the large dark olive. In common with other upwinged species, the eyes of the male are much larger than those of the female.

Kite's Imperial

Fig. 59. Oliver Kite's ever-popular Imperial.

In the 1960s Major Oliver Kite acquired a great reputation not only for his flyfishing skills but also for his ability to share with others a tremendous enthusiasm for the sport. This he did through his BBC television series, *Kite's Country*. The Imperial, devised in 1962, is a simple pattern but one which has stood the test of time. It is a sufficiently close match to the large dark olive dun that you are unlikely to need anything more complicated. Size 14 provides a good match for the large dark olive.

Grey hackle fibres make the tail, the body and thorax are of heron herl, and the hackle is honey-dun cock. (For autumn fishing, honey-dun hackles are recommended for the tails.) The tying thread is purple.

Fig. 60. The large dark olive spinner – this one is a female – is rarely seen in significant numbers on the water during the daytime.

Iron blue

(Baëtis niger, B. muticus)

Fig. 61. Iron blue dun (m)

The iron blue is the smallest upwinged fly you are likely to see in early spring. It is much darker than any of the other upwinged flies, and its wings are very dark grey.

Iron blue dun

A 'from lunch until teatime' fly, the iron blue dun first puts in an appearance in April and May, and then reappears in September, although in shady places you are quite likely to come across small numbers of these insects during the day in every month of the trout fishing season. It is strictly a river fly and occurs on chalk streams, spate rivers and fast-flowing brooks.

The iron blue dun emerges at the surface in open water, and has the reputation of hatching in bad weather; however, on many rivers the hatches can be fairly dense even on sunny spring days. Specific imitations have been devised, but a general pattern is often acceptable in the rough and tumble of a spring river.

The male and female duns of the iron blue are very similar in appearance. The females, which are generally slightly larger and stouter in the body than the males, have small, pale olive-yellow eyes and, of course, unlike the males they do not have claspers appended to the penultimate segment of the abdomen.

Magnificent Seven: Greenwell's Glory, size 16.

Iron Blue Dun (Pat Russell)

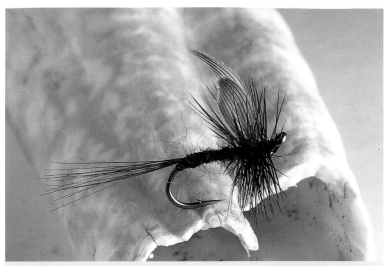

Fig. 62. Pat Russell's Iron Blue Dun.

The late Pat Russell of Romsey designed many effective dry flies which have become firm favourites with chalk-streams anglers. Several of these, including his Iron Blue Dun, are now standard patterns on many other types of river.

The tying, on a size 16 hook, is very simple. The tail is of slate-blue cock hackle fibres, the body is dark heron herl and is tipped with neon-magenta thread. The hackle is slate-blue cock. In the version illustrated, paired wings of starling have been added.

Parachute version
Pat Russell's Parachute Iron Blue Dun follows the above pattern, but the twisted heron herl body is fitted with a slate-grey parachute hackle.

Fig. 63. This Parachute version of the Iron Blue Dun was tied by Nigel Jackson of Cilgerran.

Iron blue spinner

Fig. 64. Iron blue spinner (f).

Iron blue spinners lays their eggs in the afternoon, and so they are useful flies for anglers to imitate. At this final stage in the life-cycle the differences between the sexes are quite marked. The female is sometimes called the little claret spinner, while the male has to live with the title jenny spinner.

In common with the other *baetids*, iron blue spinners are reputed always to crawl beneath the surface in order to lay their eggs. Spent female spinners may therefore be difficult to spot if they get trapped beneath the surface film. A good imitation is the Houghton Ruby.

Male spinners are most commonly found floating on the water in exposed locations during blustery weather.

Magnificent Seven, female: Greenwell's Glory, size 16
male: Tups Indispensable, size 16

Fig. 65. Iron blue spinner (m). This handsome fly is commonly referred to as the jenny spinner.

Houghton Ruby (William Lunn)

Fig. 66. The Houghton Ruby.

This is one of several classic flies devised by William Lunn, a river keeper on the Houghton Club's stretch of the River Test in the early years of the twentieth century. (Since then, two more generations of Lunns have continued the tradition and secured great reputations for their river-keeping expertise on the same fisheries.)

William Lunn was also responsible for the development of a very effective caperer sedge imitation and two other immortal patterns of upwinged flies, Lunn's Yellow Boy (a sunk *Baëtis* spinner imitation) and Lunn's Particular.

When tied on a size 16 hook, the Houghton Ruby is a first-class imitation of the female iron blue spinner.

The tail is made from three fibres of white cock hackle, and the body is a Rhode Island Red hackle stalk, dyed crimson. The wings are a pair of light blue dun hackle tips tied in the spent position, and the head is formed from crimson tying thread.

Although intended as a match for the female iron blue spinner, when trout are taking fallen male spinners of the iron blue (the jenny spinner) a Houghton Ruby will probably still be acceptable; if not, you will need an even closer imitation, for which you might like to try a size 16 Tups Indispensable.

March brown
(Rithrogena germanica)

For centuries the march brown has figured prominently in angling writing. This is rather odd because this fly is rarely seen on the majority of rivers and streams and does not appear on stillwaters.

In late March and early April the main hatches of march browns occur. Often the duns come off in waves spread over two or three hours, but it is unusual for one of these bursts of activity to last much more than fifteen minutes and I have known a hatch to take just five minutes. In deeper water trout seem to take mainly the nymphs as they ascend and struggle through the surface film, whereas in shallow stretches they are often seen rising to the floating dun.

This is a fly of the fast-flowing northern and western rivers with stony beds. March browns can be present on one river but absent from an apparently similar neighbouring one. Their distribution along a river is often patchy, and for some obscure reason they are rarely encountered on small tributary streams and brooks.

Late march brown (*Ecdyonurus venosus*)

From May onwards a very similar fly, the late march brown appears. As far as imitation is concerned, the same patterns will do for both.

Magnificent Seven: Greenwell's Glory, size 12.

Fig. 67. The River Teifi at march brown time.

The march brown nymph
(a typical stone clinger)

Fig. 68. March brown nymph.

The nymph of the march brown is a stone clinger and so it is not readily available to trout except during a hatch. March brown nymphs have a preference for the fast-flowing water of the runs and glides, unlike the agile darters, which are usually found in greatest concentration near the margins or in weed beds.

A specific imitation of the march brown nymph is unnecessary, particularly in the turbulent waters of a spate river in springtime. A size 12 GRHE (see page 47), fished just below the surface, is usually an effective nymph/emerger imitation when march browns are hatching.

Magnificent Seven: GRHE, size 12.

Fishing tip
Very often all you need do is to cast upstream and across the turbulent current, allowing your nymph to drift downstream. The conflicting surface currents of spring, pulling your leader this way and that, will impart quite enough movement to ensure that your nymph imitates the feeble swimming action of the natural march brown nymph just prior to its breaking through the surface film.

The march brown dun

Fig. 69. March brown dun (f).

With its tall mottled forewings and large hindwings, the march brown is a most striking upwinged fly. Its nymph is one of the very few stone clingers that 'hatch' in open water; the majority of its relatives emerge by crawling out via the shallows or by climbing onto partly submerged rocks.

While on the surface, march brown duns are at the mercy of wind and current; however, once airborne they seem to have an unusually good sense of direction and tend to head straight for the bank, where they cling to the first bit of firm material they can find. Tree trunks close to the surface can become dappled with duns wafting in the breeze as they complete the wing-drying process.

Magnificent Seven: Greenwell's Glory, size 12

Fig. 70. March brown dun (m).

March Brown (dry)

Fig. 71. A March Brown dry fly.

This fly, based on a hatching dun, was devised by W H Lawrie. The tail is a few honey-dun cock fibres, the body is a dubbed mixture of yellow seal's fur and hare's ear ribbed with fine gold wire, and the wing is hen pheasant. A henny brown hackle and a head formed from the yellow tying thread complete the dressing. A hackled version of this fly is equally effective, but in the turbulent waters of a spring spate river the wings do make the fly much easier to see.

Fishing tip
If you apply floatant to this fly it will sit reasonably high upon the surface; however, when fished without having been treated with floatant it soon sinks into the surface film and is an effective imitation of the emerging march brown dun.

Fig. 72. March brown spinners deposit their eggs on the water surface late in the day, rarely causing a rise. If required, a size 12 Pheasant Tail Spinner would be a suitable imitation.

Olive upright

(Rithrogena semicolorata)

Fig. 73. Olive upright dun (f).

This close cousin of the march brown is a fly of swift rocky streams, but it is also to be found in the riffles on many lowland rivers. The nymph is one of the stone clingers. The olive upright is extremely sensitive to water pollution, and is therefore an indicator of water quality.

The olive upright dun

Water temperature greatly affects the rate of development of olive upright nymphs, and so their hatching period can vary significantly from year to year depending on the weather. Usually the peak of the hatch occurs in May and June, and duns are to be seen both in the morning and in the evening. It is in heavy evening hatches that trout can become totally preoccupied with olive upright duns, and a close imitation is then the only way of getting results.

Fig. 74. Olive upright dun (m).

Olive Upright (Guy Mawle)

Fig. 75. Olive Upright, tied by Guy Mawle.

In 1982, Guy Mawle worked with friends on the River Usk to devise this specific imitation of the olive upright dun. The Usk often has dense hatches of this fly on May, June and July afternoons and evenings, and the trout can become extremely selective.

A size 14 long-shank hook is used. The tying thread is primrose, and this is an important feature of the underbody. The tail, which should be tied short, is of grizzle hackle fibres from a spade hackle, and the slim, lightly dubbed body uses a mixture of cream, some yellow and rather less olive seal fur and is ribbed with gold wire. The wings are light blue dun hackle points and the hackle is three turns of grizzle cock. Omitting the wings does appear to detract from the effectiveness of this fly.

When treated with floatant, or when dampened by water, the body of the Olive Upright darkens quite noticeably; the one in the illustration was photographed while it was wet.

Fishing tip
This fly is most effective when fished on a leader with a fine tippet – 2–3 lb breaking strain should be ideal provided your rod is sufficiently light to absorb most of the shock as you tighten into a fish.

The olive upright spinner

Fig. 76. Olive upright spinner (f).

This spinner, commonly called the yellow upright, is to be seen swarming above the water from mid-afternoon onwards. It is usually late in the day when the females lay their eggs; this they do by alighting on emergent rocks or vegetation and dipping their ovipositors into the water, and so it is mainly the spent yellow upright spinners, male and female, which trout are able to take.

Guy Mawle's Olive Upright (page 71) is a suitable imitation for late-evening fishing when both duns and spinners are on the water. Do not add floatant to the fly, and cast a little more heavily than you would when fishing the dun so that your fly is made to sink into the surface film rather than letting it float high upon its hackle tips.

Magnificent Seven: Tups Indispensable, size 12.

Fig. 77. Male yellow upright spinners swarm over the water on exposed upland streams, and on breezy evenings they end up on the water in fair numbers.

Yellow may

(Heptagenia sulphurea)

Fig. 78. Yellow may dun (f).

The nymph of the yellow may is another of the stone clingers and is far more common on spate rivers than on chalk streams. The main hatch usually begins in the second half of May and continues through June and well into July.

The yellow may dun

The duns, with their brilliant sulphur yellow wings, are easily recognised at a distance. They hatch in open water from mid-morning onwards, and numbers increase towards dusk. Although there are rarely sufficient yellow may duns on the surface to cause a selective rise, trout are certainly willing to take them along with whatever else is available. A specific imitation for matching both the dun and the spinner is described on page 75.

Magnificent Seven: Tups Indispensable, size 12.

Fig. 79. Yellow may dun (m).

The yellow may spinner

Fig. 80. Yellow may spinner (f).

On warm evenings from sunset until dusk the female spinners of the yellow may return to the water to lay their eggs. Flies which trickled off as duns over a period of many hours now appear *en masse*, and on some spate rivers the result is a most selective evening rise. Any yellow may duns on the water at that time are given the same treatment as the spinners, and their numbers are very much thinned out by leaping trout.

On the limestone rivers of Ireland and the chalk streams of southern England, yellow mays are rarely seen in great numbers and trout do not seem to become preoccupied with them; indeed, I have observed them being studiously ignored by trout rising steadily to pale wateries and blue-winged olive spinners.

Magnificent Seven: Tups Indispensable, size 12.

Fig. 81. Yellow may spinner (m).

Yellow May (Mike Weaver)

Fig. 82. Yellow May Sparkle Dun, tied by Mike Weaver.

Mike Weaver, who has spent many years researching and fishing on the rivers of the West Country as well as further afield, rates the yellow may dun and its spinner as extremely important angling flies on those spate rivers where it occurs in good numbers. His Yellow May patterns are well tried and tested, and this is one of the finest.

The tying details are as follows: the hook should be a standard size 16, such as Partridge L3A, the tying thread may be either yellow or cream, and the tail is golden-yellow Lureflash Antron body wool. The body of the fly is dubbed with SLF, colour code MC7, and the wings are made of deer-hair in a light natural shade similar to honey dun. The wings are flared through 180 degrees.

Use this fly when trout are rising to yellow may duns or spinners.

Fig. 83. An alternative yellow may, the Thorax Hackle Dun also tied by Mike Weaver, uses the same SLF body, a honey-dun hackle and a few of the same hackle fibres for the tail.

Large brook

(Ecdyonurus torrentis)

Fig. 84. Large brook dun (f).

The large brook dun

The large brook dun is a fly of fast, boulder-strewn rivers and streams, and it is most abundant from late April until mid-June. The nymph is a stone clinger which hatches mainly by crawling onto exposed stones; however, a significant proportion may hatch at the surface in mid-stream. At times of peak emergence trout feed with enthusiasm on these duns, and windborne casualties add to the feast on blustery days. Rises to this dun can be selective, probably because of their large size.

Even in a dense hatch, a specific imitation does not seem to be necessary provided you use a fly of comparable size and roughly the right colour. A March Brown will generally do the trick.

Magnificent Seven: Greenwell's Glory, size 12.

Fig. 85. Large brook dun (m).

The large brook spinner

Fig. 86. Large brook spinner (f).

The large brook spinner is sometimes referred to as the large red spinner, a name it shares with the march brown, the autumn dun and the late march brown.

Large brook spinners are flies of the late afternoon and early evening. They lay their eggs by dipping down onto the water surface. The eggs are released in small batches. Male spinners of this species swarm along the edge of the water and some must fall victim to trout; however, as male and female spinners are very similar in appearance one fly pattern will do for both.

No specific imitation is necessary, as a size 12 dry March Brown (particularly useful when both duns and spinners are on the water) or a large Pheasant Tail Spinner seem to work just fine.

Magnificent Seven: Greenwell's Glory, size 12.

Fig. 87. Large brook spinner (m).

Claret

(Leptophlebia vespertina)

The claret dun is mainly a fly of the stillwaters, but it does also occur in some of the slower-flowing rivers. It is a very dark fly and is sometimes confused with the iron blue dun. These flies are easily distinguished, however, because the claret duns and spinners each have three tails while iron blues have just two.

The main hatches occur in May and June, but sometimes a reasonably good hatch will continue into July. The adults appear during the day, generally from around noon onwards.

The claret dun occurs in great numbers on some small stillwaters in the south and west of England. It is also quite common in Scottish lochs and Welsh llyns, and is plentiful in Ireland's moorland loughs. This fly is also to be found in boggy bays on some of the limestone lakes of central Ireland. Although rarely seen in large quantities on lowland rivers, claret duns are found in many upland streams, particularly in areas where the land is moderately acidic.

Sepia dun and spinner *(Leptophlebia marginata)*

The sepia dun is found in similar habitats to the claret. The wings of this rather uncommon upwinged fly are more brown than those of the claret, but for all practical purposes it can be considered as a claret as far as the flyfisher is concerned.

Fig. 88. Llyn Berwen, where claret duns are plentiful.

The claret nymph
(a typical laboured swimmer)

Fig. 89. A claret nymph near to hatching.

Although slightly flattened, these reddish-brown nymphs are in other respects quite similar in appearance to the darker of the 'olive' nymphs. The claret nymph has prominent gill filaments along the sides of its body, and the tails are unusually long and are spread very widely apart.

Claret nymphs belong to the laboured swimmer group and spend most of their time among stones, mosses and debris, preferring places where the bottom is muddy. They move much more slowly than the agile-darting nymphs and rarely leave the bed of the lake or river unless they are ready to hatch. When ready to hatch into duns, claret nymphs swim up to the surface.

Magnificent Seven: A GRHE (page 47) is an adequate match for the claret nymph; however, if you want a closer imitation then you could try tying up a few Pheasant Tail Nymphs (page 206) with widely spread tail whisks.

Fishing tip
It is important to retrieve your nymph slowly: claret nymphs are not particularly energetic creatures.

The claret dun

Fig. 90. Claret dun (f).

The adult claret dun and its spinner each have three tails, and at both of these winged stages in the life-cycle the differences between males and females are minimal as far as matching the hatch is concerned. The pale hindwings of the claret dun are a distinguishing feature which is quite noticeable even at a distance of several yards.

Claret duns emerge in open water, generally near the edge of the lake, in late spring. The peak of the hatch usually occurs between mid-May and the end of June. With duns coming off from early afternoon until well into the evening, it is not unusual to have claret duns and spinners on the water at the same time.

Magnificent Seven: Greenwell's Glory, size 14.

Fig. 91. Claret dun (m).

Claret Dun (J R Harris)

Fig. 92. J R Harris' Claret Dun.

Irish angler-entomologist J R Harris devised this very simple but effective tying of the Claret Dun. I know of none better.

J R Harris was both a skilled angler and a scientific naturalist, and in 1952 he applied both of these abilities to produce a very fine book, *The Angler's Entomology*; it is still one of the finest studies of the angler's flies yet produced. In his book, Harris not only described the habitat, hatching times and behaviour of most of the important natural flies, but he also included several of his own artificial fly patterns, of which his Claret Dun and Claret Spinner have remained firm favourites with many anglers for almost half a century.

The Claret Dun uses claret tying thread (what else?), dark blue dun cock hackle fibres for the tail, dark heron herl, dyed claret, for the body, which should be ribbed with fine gold wire, and finally a dark blue-dun cock hackle clipped with a V cut underneath – a feature copied to advantage in several more recently developed patterns.

As an alternative to the heron herl, a mixture of claret mohair and mole's fur is sometimes used as the body dubbing.

Wet fly alternative
In choppy waters, some claret duns inevitably capsize and are drowned. A size 14 Mallard and Claret fished very slowly just below the surface is a useful wet fly imitation in these circumstances.

The claret spinner

Fig. 93. Claret spinner (f).

The claret duns become spinners some distance from the water, and the males tend to swarm around trees or bushes near the edge of the lake. Only infrequently are male spinners seen on the water in any quantity, and so it is mainly the egg-laying females and the spent female spinners which contribute to the evening rise. In any case, the male and female spinners are quite similar, and a special imitation of the male is not justified.

Female claret spinners fly out across the lake to lay their eggs in small batches. This they do by dipping periodically onto the surface until finally they fall as spent flies. Unless the weather is unseasonably cold, a resulting evening rise can be expected.

Magnificent Seven: Greenwell's Glory, size 14.

Fig. 94. Claret spinner (m).

Pheasant Tail Spinner

Fig. 95. Pheasant Tail Spinner.

As a representation of the claret spinner or the sepia spinner the Pheasant Tail Spinner will invariably pass muster, which is probably why there are so few specific patterns for imitating these particular spinners and none which has gained widespread popularity.

This is a very old pattern and dates back to the turn of the century. The hook size is usually 12 or 14, and the tying thread brown. A tail of honey dun cock fibres is used, and the body is of cock pheasant tail fibres ribbed with fine gold wire. The Pheasant Tail Spinner is most often tied with just a honey dun cock hackle, but hackle-tip spent wings of rusty dun or bright blue are sometimes added.

This fly will represent fairly well any of the dark upwinged spinners. In an emergency, it will even do service as a march brown dun!

Fishing tip
Claret spinners lay their eggs by dipping down onto the surface, and so a useful tactic is to cast your dry fly so that it alights beside and slightly behind a surface-feeding trout. The reflex reaction of the fish is to turn and seize the fly before it can take off again. The advantage of this approach is that the trout has virtually no chance of seeing your leader: a useful tactic for fooling a hyper-cautious fish.

Turkey brown

(Paraleptophlebia submarginata)

Fig. 96. Turkey brown dun (f).

This is a fly found on the slower reaches of lowland spate rivers and rough streams of the West Country, Wales and the north of England, but it is not frequently encountered on the chalk streams of southern England or on the limestone rivers of Ireland. Although it occurs quite widely the hatches are extremely sparse, and so there is very little prospect of trout selecting this fly in preference to any other species available at the time.

Turkey brown nymphs are larger than, but otherwise similar to, claret nymphs. They are laboured swimmers and are found among marginal weeds and in the debris which collects in back eddies.

The duns hatch at the surface during the daytime in May, June and early July, but on any particular river they usually have a short season which usually lasts no more than four weeks. The spinners are rarely to be seen on the water during daylight hours. The body of the female spinner is a mid-brown and the male a more ruddy brown; both have clear wings.

In the unlikely event that you require to match reasonably accurately either the dun or the spinner, a size 12 Pheasant Tail Spinner should suffice.

Magnificent Seven (dun and spinner): Greenwell's Glory, size 12.

Mayfly

(Ephemera danica, E. vulgata)

This is the biggest and best known of the upwinged flies, and its appearance causes great excitement among trout and trout fishers alike. The differences between the two common British species are minimal as far as anglers (and fish) are concerned.

The mayfly season has long been called 'duffer's fortnight' – the implication being that trout become almost suicidal when these large flies are about. In practice, this is not always the case, and mayfly fishing can be a most frustrating experience. Partly this may be because flyfishers who, in the weeks before the mayfly hatch, have been catching trout on small flies do not wait long enough before tightening after the take.

The most commonly occuring mayfly is *Ephemera danica* and it is found in greatest numbers in alkaline or neutral lakes and rivers, although it is also common in slightly acidic waters. *Ephemera vulgata* is more frequently encountered in mildly acidic lowland streams and seems to have a more extended season of emergence. This less common mayfly species is, on average, slightly smaller and its dun is rather darker than *Ephemera danica.* The differences are more easily seen at the spinner stage, where *E. vulgata* tends to have an olive tinge rather than the pale cream abdomen of *E. danica.*

Fig. 97. Ireland's Lough Sheelin has an excellent mayfly hatch.

The mayfly nymph
(a burrower)

Fig. 98. Mayfly nymph.

Living in tunnels in the beds of rivers and lakes, mayfly nymphs have specially adapted breathing filaments which they wave back and forth to create a current over their backs. By means of these filaments the nymphs extract oxygen from static water. When the river-bed sand and gravel become compacted, mayfly numbers decline. A useful spin-off from work to rehabilitate spawning gravels is that the habitat may also become more suitable for mayflies and other bottom-burrowing creatures on which young trout and salmon feed.

The body of the male nymph is generally little more than two thirds as long as that of the female, which can reach 30 mm. It is not uncommon to see some much smaller adult mayflies towards the end of the main hatch.

The developing nymphs, which normally take at least two years to reach maturity, burrow beneath gravel and silt and are rarely accessible to trout. The mature nymphs emerge from the bed of the lake or river and migrate towards shallower water. Mayfly nymphs normally crawl fairly slowly, but when necessary they are able to swim quickly with an undulating motion. They are at their most vulnerable when they begin ascending to the surface to hatch.

Magnificent Seven: Damsel Nymph, size 10.

Mayfly Nymph (Peter Masters)

Fig. 99. Mayfly Nymph, tied by Peter Masters.

Of all the mayfly nymphs ever devised, the pattern developed by that innovative genius, Richard Walker, is surely the most widely used. And rightly so, for when tied properly (shop-bought versions are often far too bulky) it is a very good imitation of the mature mayfly nymph. This variation, developed by Peter Masters, broadly follows Walker's recipe, but has the refinement of nylon legs and llama-wool body ribbed with brown thread. The tail and the wing covers are made from pheasant-tail fibres, and the hackle is grizzle cock, dyed yellow.

Fishing tips
When fishing on rivers a size 10 or even a 12 is usually best. Cast upstream and across and allow the nymph to sink. When your nymph nears the lie of a trout, make a long steady pull on the line so that the nymph swims towards the surface as if ascending to hatch.

On lakes, use on a long leader. Cast out and allow the nymph to sink to the bottom. Make a slow figure-of-eight retrieve until the nymph nears a trout (or where you expect one to be); then retrieve more rapidly so that the nymph rises towards the surface. If you see a fish following the nymph, do not slow down the retrieve or it will probably shy away. Instead, speed up slightly and you may trigger a lunging take.

The mayfly dun

Fig. 100. Mayfly dun, *Ephemera danica* (f).

The main hatch usually begins somewhere between mid-May and the first week of June, but there are regional variations. A cold winter can delay the mayfly season by two or three weeks, while following a mild winter it is possible to begin mayfly fishing as early as the last week of April.

The hatch generally begins early in the afternoon and continues for several hours. In drizzly weather mayfly duns can drift and flutter on the surface for up to two minutes before taking flight to nearby vegetation, whereas on bright days the duns get airborne more quickly, so that fewer are taken by the trout, and they generally head for high resting places which are well out of reach.

The female mayfly dun has a body typically 25 mm long, although specimens as small as 15 mm and as large as 30 mm are not uncommon. The male mayfly dun is typically only two thirds the size of the female; however, apart from having a pair of claspers appended from the penultimate segment of the abdomen and somewhat larger eyes than its mate, the male is very similar indeed to the female.

Magnificent Seven: Greenwell's Glory, size 10.

Mayfly Dun (Peter Masters)

Fig. 101. Peter Masters' deer-hair Mayfly Dun.

This deer-hair pattern has fooled some very wary trout on hard-fished waters. It is also remarkably durable for such a large fly.

The tying is fairly straightforward and combines modern plastics with highly buoyant deerhair. The hook is a size 12 and the tying thread is brown. The tail and body are deer hair, dyed yellow, the body being barred with tying thread. This mayfly sports a yellow plastic dun wing from Roman Moser. A grizzle hackle, dyed yellow, and a small whip-finish head complete the fly.

Fishing tips
Trout are sometimes a little wary of large duns that suddenly fall from the sky, so it usually pays to cast well upstream of a rising fish (but keeping the fly line well clear of the target zone, of course) so that your fly drifts across the trout's window in the same way that most of the natural duns will be doing.

With such large flies, it is very easy to tighten up too soon, especially in a heavy hatch when trout lie just below the surface and poke their heads up leisurely to take the mayfly duns. The timing of the 'strike' has to be varied according to the average size of the trout. Large fish need to be given more time to turn their heads down, and so you will need to wait that much longer before tightening up.

The mayfly spinner

Fig. 102. Mayfly spinner (f).

Swarms of male spinners form cloud columns, usually within a stone's throw of the waterside. There they climb and dive until a female flies into the swarm and mates. After mating the paired flies head off towards the water, but generally during the journey the male will fall to the ground. Egg-laying mayfly spinners fly a foot or so above the surface (generally upstream on rivers) touching down periodically to release a batch of eggs. Once all of their eggs have been expended, the spinners soon tire and fall to the surface, where they flutter awhile before dying in the 'spent gnat' position.

The female is of most interest to anglers, although on breezy days many of the males end up on the water, too.

Magnificent Seven: Tups Indispensable, size 10.

Fig. 103. Mayfly spinner (m).

No Hook Spinner

Fig. 104. No Hook Spinner, tied by John Riegen.

This is a fly born out of frustration with some highly educated brown trout which refused conventional patterns. By clipping off the hook bend and using a very fine leader it was occasionally possible to overcome their paranoia. So John Riegen and I devised a spent spinner with no visible hook. It achieves the objectives of floating, being castable without spinning the leader, and tempting fussy trout.

The body is of hollow deer-hair fibres ribbed with brown tying thread. The tail is also deer-hair, and the wings are formed from polypropylene floating yarn. The detached body is not tied in line with the hook but at right angles to it, and so the hook is concealed within the wings. A spot of Superglue where the hook, wings and body meet ensures that the hook does not rotate relative to the fly body. Do not let the glue run up the body or wing material or they will become stiff and reduce the chances of a fish being hooked.

Fishing tips
The best way to make your fly mimic a dead mayfly is to do absolutely nothing. On a lake this is easy, but on flowing water it means casting in such a way as to minimise drag. For this, the wiggle cast is a useful technique. The No Hook Spinner has a large contact area which also reduces drag when fishing in turbulent water.

Grannom

(*Brachycentrus subnubilis*)

Fig. 105. A grannom sedge.

In spring, the first sedge fly of real importance to river fishers is the grannom, and in areas where it occurs this smallish sedge fly causes great excitement both on chalk streams and on rain-fed rivers. The grannom appears in April and the main hatch usually lasts for ten days or so, with flies coming off the water from mid-morning until late afternoon. In damp weather the adults often fall back to the surface several times before reaching the safety of bankside vegetation, and it is not uncommon to see a trout leap from the water several times in an attempt to seize a newly emerged grannom sedge.

The grannom seems to prefer medium-paced rivers and streams, but it is also found on some slow-flowing chalk streams. This is not a fly of the mountain torrents, and it is rarely reported from stillwaters except in the vicinity of inflowing streams. Grannom sedges generally hatch from the shallower water, giving the fish little time to intercept the ascending pupae, but the hatching pupa struggling to free itself from its pupal case is equally as acceptable a morsel as the winged adult. Trout tend to ignore small upwinged flies when the grannom is on the water, but as other sedges are rare at that time a close imitation is probably unnecessary: any small sedge will do.

Magnificent Seven: Silver Sedge, size 14.

Grannom (Pat Russell)

Fig. 106. Pat Russell's Grannom.

This very popular and successful pattern was devised by Romsey fly dresser Pat Russell who fished with it extensively on the chalk streams of southern England. It is generally tied only on a size 14 hook because the grannom, like most sedge flies, varies little in size from one individual to another.

The fly illustrated above was tied by Nigel Jackson, a close friend of the late Pat Russell. Because it is meant to represent a sedge fly there is, of course, no tail on this pattern. Few sedge patterns are simpler to tie or more effective in use. The tying thread is green, and a tip of fluorescent green wool is tied in before the body of heron herl. (This green tip is meant to represent the egg ball carried by the female grannom after mating, but the fly works very well as an imitation of the hatching grannom sedge.) The wing is of blue dun cock hackle fibres clipped off level with the hook bend. Finally, a hackle of ginger cock is added before a whip-finished head.

Fishing tip
On chalk streams, the grannom larvae are often to be found in greatest concentrations in and around weed beds, whereas on stony spate rivers the swift glides are usually good places to fish during a grannom hatch.

Yellow spotted sedge

(Philopotamus montanus)

Fig. 107. Yellow spotted sedge.

This and a number of similar yellow spotted, dark-winged sedges begin hatching towards the end of spring, and the adults generally emerge from early afternoon onwards. There is also a group of sedge flies with lighter brown wings spotted with yellow, and various writers including Taff Price have chosen to differentiate between these yellow spotted paler sedges and the somewhat larger and darker yellow spotted sedges. Both of these groups are to be found on small rivers and streams, and in spring substantial swarms can sometimes be seen on heavily wooded sections of lowland streams. The yellow spotted sedge, *Philopotamus montanus*, seems to have a particular preference for fast-flowing wooded streams and torrents through steep ravines.

For angling purposes, a specific imitation of any of the spotted sedges seems to be quite unnecessary because trout would appear willing to accept pretty well any sedge-shaped fly of about the right size provided it is presented in a realistic way. A Grannom or small deer-hair sedge should serve very well whenever you need a general representation of the medium-sized sedge flies of spring.

Magnificent Seven: Silver Sedge, size 14.

Black sedge

(Silo nigricornis)

Fig. 108. Black sedge.

The black sedges, of which there are several species, are in the main flies of rivers and streams. In May and early June they can be seen swirling around just above the surface in swarms of a few dozen at a time. Occasionally a collision occurs, but as they are rarely seen in blustery weather it seems as if they are intent upon minimising casualties of this type.

Black sedges are most plentiful from mid-afternoon onwards, and the best dry-fly fishing is often towards the end of the day. Earlier on, a sedge pupa imitation offered in regions where the black sedges are seen swarming will sometimes produce good results even though there is no significant rise.

A dark deer-hair sedge can be expected to work well when black sedges are swarming beneath the trees, but if on occasions you find black sedges about and you have no suitable imitation, try a large black gnat. Indeed, on one occasion on a small Irish stream a lowly Hawthorn Fly served as a very effective substitute for a dark sedge: the colour and size were about right, and the hungry trout were in too much of a hurry to bother about the shape of the meal.

Magnificent Seven: Silver Sedge, size 14.

February red

(*Taeniopteryx nebulosa, Brachyptera risi*)

Fig. 109. February red.

Despite its common name, this little fly is generally seen in greatest numbers in March and April. February red is a name that anglers in some parts of the British Isles give to all of the reddish-brown stoneflies of spring. In most areas this particular stonefly occurs in only moderate numbers and tends to be ignored by trout when there are upwinged flies on the water.

Unusually for a stonefly the February red is most frequently found in slow-flowing stretches of spate rivers and in weedy lowland streams. This fly is not normally encountered in significant quantities on the southern chalk streams.

In those places where spring stonefly hatches are dense, the February red and any other medium-sized stoneflies are worth imitating with a spidery pattern of the right size and colour, fished awash in the surface film or just beneath the surface to represent the drowning insect. The Snipe and Purple, which may be fished to good effect either wet, swamped ('damp') or dry, is a good general pattern to represent this or any other of the medium-sized brown stoneflies.

The nymphs of the small and medium-sized stoneflies of spring are adequately imitated with a weighted Pheasant Tail Nymph.

Magnificent Seven: Coch-y-bonddu, size 14.

Snipe and Purple

Fig. 110. Snipe and Purple.

This is a traditional North Country imitation of the drowned iron blue, but it is also a very useful fly when medium-sized stoneflies such as the February red are being blown onto the water in springtime.

The tying is very straightforward, and so this is an ideal fly pattern for anyone just beginning fly dressing. It can be tied on a range of hook sizes, and 12 to 16 should prove most useful. The body is of purple silk, and the hackle is of dark snipe, which should be tied very sparse.

North Country spider patterns such as this are generally used as wet flies, often on a multi-fly leader. Less commonly, but just as effectively, they are treated with floatant and fished in the surface film. This is a great tactic when stoneflies are on the water.

Once you have seen a drowning stonefly with its four slim wings stuck in the surface film, you will probably agree that the Snipe and Purple is actually quite a good imitation of the February red and the other medium brown stoneflies which appear early in the season. But tied in the smaller sizes, this fly also serves as a pretty good general representation of many of the autumn stoneflies, including the willow fly and the needle fly.

Large stonefly

(Perlodes microcephala)

Fig. 111. Large stonefly nymph.

This large fly or one of its close relatives would surely create real interest in the trout world if only it hatched in batches and appeared in larger numbers at the surface; unfortunately, although they are very common in many rivers, the large stonefly nymphs live beneath stones and hatch into winged adults by crawling onto exposed rocks in the shallows. It is difficult to mimic this behaviour with an artificial fly and not get snagged on the river bed.

The large stonefly nymph

Large stonefly nymphs seem to prefer well-oxygenated water, and in warm weather they often congregate in the fast riffles. They are also intolerant of pollution, and so an abundance of stonefly nymphs is an indicator of high water quality.

These mayfly-sized nymphs are slow-growing creatures and they take two years or more to reach maturity, unlike many of the smaller species which have a one-year life-cycle. Trout rummage among the smaller stones to disturb stonefly nymphs from their hideouts, but the nymphs of the large stonefly almost invariably select large, dark-coloured stones under which to live, achieving a degree of camouflage as well as the added security of a strong front door.

Magnificent Seven: GRHE, size 8 or 10.

Large Stonefly Creeper (Peter Masters)

Fig. 112. Large Stonefly Creeper, tied by Peter Masters.

Fly dressers sometimes delight in constructing realistic copies of the large stonefly nymph, complete with wing cases, jointed legs, tails and antennae. Most of these models, skilfully built though they are, would remain rigid when towed through the water, and so they would not be truly lifelike.

Peter Masters ties a Large Stonefly Nymph which is a generally acceptable (to a hungry trout) copy of the real thing, and when it is retrieved slowly through the water the legs move in a credible way.

The hook is a size 8 low-water salmon iron, and black tying thread is used. For the tails and also for the antennae, Peter uses 25-lb b.s. clear monofilament nylon. The body and thorax are made by dubbing brown Antron of a shade to match the natural insects, the legs are partridge body feather (a grouse body feather is also suitable), and the wing case and back of the abdomen are brown Raffene ribbed with 10-lb b.s. clear monofilament nylon.

Although it is rather a time-consuming process, it is possible to tie this nymph in various sizes and various shades of brown and grey (the colours of most stonefly nymphs) to match a range of natural stonefly creepers.

The large stonefly adult

Fig. 113. Large stonefly (f).

These meaty mouthfuls appear on the trout's menu from the end of March until the middle of June, with the peak of the hatch usually occurring in May. The males have very short wings and are unable to fly, and so they are to be found sunning themselves on rocks, tree trunks and fencing posts beside the river while the females go about the business of courting and egg-laying.

Mating is completed on the ground, and then the females fly across the river and dip down to lay their eggs. Spent females do not always end up on the water but those that do tend to put up quite a struggle, which inevitably attracts the attention of trout.

Magnificent Seven: Coch-y-bonddu, size 10.

Fig. 114. The male large stonefly has very short wings and cannot fly. The females do the courting.

Large Stonefly (Melvin Grey)

Fig. 115. Large Stonefly, tied by Melvin Grey.

Once a large stonefly has released all her eggs and lies struggling in the surface, trout are only too pleased to administer the last rites. It makes sense to use an artificial fly of more or less the right size, shape and colour, and it is for that reason that Melvin Grey has devised this general imitation.

The hook is a long-shank size 12, and the tying thread is brown. The legs are made from pheasant-tail fibres, which are knotted to represent the joints and then tied in at right angles to the hook shank. Then the tails and antennae are added; these are made from goose-wing feather fibres tied in so that they curve outwards. The body can then be dubbed on using dark brown SLF.

Once the body of the stonefly has been completed, it is overlaid with a pair of polythene wings cut from a heavy-duty fertiliser bag. The wings can be veined using an indelible pen if you so wish (although it is debatable whether a trout would appreciate this detail even if the wing veins were visible from under the water). Veniard's dark brown Body Stretch is used for the thorax.

Fishing tip
This is a fly for fishing *in* the surface rather than on it. Do not bother to apply floatant unless you intend fishing in very turbulent water.

Black midge

(*Chironomus* species)

Fig. 116. An adult black midge.

Of the more than 400 chironomid midges which are found in the British Isles, many are so small that it is impractical to imitate them with an artificial fly. (That is not to say that trout always ignore the micro-midges, of course!) Flyfishers are generally interested in copying the larger midges, with body lengths from 5 to 12 mm.

Some of the very first midges to hatch are medium-sized, very dark ones. On the Irish limestone lakes they emerge in great quantities throughout the day in late March and early April, and they cause the first significant surface activity. A few weeks later, larger and rather greyer midges are seen on most large stillwaters towards the end of the afternoon. In the wind-swept waters of a large stillwater in spring-time, close imitation is not necessary, and any dark fly of the right size and more or less the right shape seems to do the trick.

Both of these midges are reported to go through several life-cycles during the year – as indeed most of the chironomids seem to do – and so moderate hatches can occur at any time during the flyfishing season.

Magnificent Seven: Olive Suspender Buzzer, size 12.

Duck Fly

Fig. 117. An emerger version of the Duck Fly.

On Ireland's famous Loch Corrib fishery, the Duck Fly season is eagerly awaited. A team of these small wet flies, fished on a longish leader, will bring up from the depths some remarkably acrobatic wild trout. And there are many other stillwaters in England, Scotland, Wales and Ireland where the same tactics are used to good effect. Trout often intercept the midge pupae and the emerging adults as they struggle to break through the surface film. Duck Flies are often tied as emergers, even though they are sometimes fished a little way under the surface.

The version of the Duck Fly illustrated here is usually tied on a size 12 or 14 Yorkshire Sedge hook. The tying thread is black. Goose herls, dyed black, are used to form the abdomen and the thorax, and the wings are a pair of white hen hackle tips.

The abdomens of chironomid midges have seven segments. Although it is clear that trout cannot count, it seems a sensible idea to tie artificial flies with a similar number.

Fishing tip
When there is a good wave on the water, long casting is unnecessary provided you avoid scaring the trout by standing up or by banging your feet against the sides of the boat.

Hawthorn fly

(Bibio marci)

Fig. 118. Hawthorn fly.

The first of the terrestrial insects to cause a worthwhile rise are the hawthorn flies. They occur throughout the British Isles. On sunny spring days, hawthorn flies flit along the hedgerows and among low bushes, and if there is a good breeze, particularly on exposed upland streams and lakes, very many of these large flies end up on the water. The large female hawthorn flies begin hatching around St Mark's Day which is 25 April, although their smaller mates are sometimes seen a week or so earlier. The hatch is generally over by mid-May.

In meadowland you will often see swarms of hawthorn flies rushing about just above head height. Once on the water, it is rare for a hawthorn fly to escape the attention of trout – indeed, this fly will often tempt the biggest trout into making a rare excursion to the surface. A splashy rise ensues, and sometimes this is coincident with a clash of trout heads.

Heather fly *(Bibio pomonae)*

A close relative of the hawthorn fly is the heather fly, which appears in late summer and autumn. In appearance it differs from the hawthorn only in having red thighs rather than being all black.

Magnificent Seven: Coch-y-bonddu, size 12.

Hawthorn Fly (Jon Beer)

Fig. 119. Jon Beer's Hawthorn Fly.

This simple but very effective pattern was devised by writer and broadcaster Jon Beer, for whom the hawthorn fly is a firm favourite. The hook is Partridge GRS3A, size 14, and the tying thread is black.

The body is black deer-hair tied in butt end near the eye (the thin end of deer-hair is not hollow) and then wrapped with turns of thread down to the bend. This gives bulk, for buoyancy. The thread is then taken to within 3 mm of the eye, the hair is pulled towards the eye and tied in, like a deer hair beetle. Trim the ends. The legs are two knotted black hackle stalks. The wings are vinyl repair patch – soft but strong and nicely patterned. They should be folded and cut with shaped wing cutters to create the shape shown in Fig. 119.

Now place the opened wings lengthways on top of the body, and fold at the tying thread (3mm from the eye). Make one turn of the thread and then fold the front half back and slightly offset. Tie down on top to give the pair of wings. The hackle is black cock.

To make a version to represent the heather fly, include one turn of a small, red cock hackle before tying in the main black hackle.

Fishing tip
Although stillwater trout will take a 'retrieved' Hawthorn Fly fished just below the surface, dry-fly tactics are usually best when tackling river trout (and 'educated' stillwater trout).

Black gnat

(Bibio johannis)

Fig. 120. One of the many flies that anglers call the black gnat.

Anglers apply the name black gnat to several species of flies of terrestrial origin that live near water and feature on the trout's menu. In spring, and again in autumn, black gnats can be seen swarming near the surface. Although the spring and autumn flies are not the same species, they are so similar that for angling purposes we can treat them as one.

For the lake fisher, the black gnat is an insect of the margins, often preferring the shade beneath overhanging trees. Any darkish dry fly of the right size (16 or 18) is usually acceptable provided it is fished on a fine leader.

On rivers and streams, black gnat clouds are frequently densest over the slower sections. Some species of 'black gnats' swarm very close to the surface, while others congregate in columns rising to above head height. Mating pairs are particularly vulnerable in blustery weather and fall to the surface, where the trout are only too pleased to consume the consumating couple. Many black gnat patterns are available, including the Knotted Midge which imitates the mating pair. Winged versions are 'bi-visible' flies: they can be seen easily on water reflecting either the sky or the bank.

Magnificent Seven: Coch-y-bonddu, size 16.

Black Gnat (Peter O'Reilly)

Fig. 121. Black Gnat, tied by Peter O'Reilly.

Traditional slim-bodied black gnats tied upwing style are usually good enough for upland trout fishing, but on calm lowland rivers and lakes a better imitation generally pays dividends. This more realistic pattern, with a bit of body bulk, was devised by Peter O'Reilly. Unlike some shop-bought black gnats it has, quite rightly, no tail. The hook is a size 16 Kamosan B170, and black tying thread should be used.

The tying is very simple, consisting of a tag of silver mylar, a body of bronze peacock herl, and a black cock hackle. A small whip-finished head completes the fly.

Mating midges, sometimes referred to as knotted midges, are particularly prone to taking a cold bath if the wind is gusty. A variation of the Black Gnat has a second hackle tied in at the hook bend and represents the tail-to-tail pair.

Fishing tip
If you have difficulty trying to keep sight of tiny dark flies such as this on the water, try adding a pair of white wings. (Tie them swept back along the fly, not upright.) The result is a 'bi-visible' fly.

Alder

(Sialis lutaria, Sialis fuliginosa)

Fig. 122. Alder larva.

Shaped very much like a sedge fly but with brittle wings like a stonefly, the alder fly has for many centuries been discussed in angling books, and yet the success of imitations of this fly is difficult to explain. Alder larvae inhabit the depths of stillwaters and the muddy backwaters of rivers, where they prey on other insects. In spring the larvae crawl ashore and pupate in the weedy margins.

The larvae are most active in April and May, and the adult is seen on the wing in greatest numbers from May until mid-June.

Alder flies lay their eggs on the underside of overhanging vegetation. There the eggs incubate and the young larvae emerge to drop into the water and scurry down to the bottom, where they spend the majority of their adolescence tunnelling in the silt. The larvae, which take two years to reach maturity, are rarely to be seen until April, when they more actively patrol the bed of the lake or river.

Winged alders, while somewhat erratic in flight, must feature only infrequently in the trout's diet. For those occasions when alder flies are about in good numbers, any dark sedge pattern ought to do the trick.

The alder larva is most definitely worthy of imitation.

Magnificent Seven (larva only): GRHE, size 12.

Fig. 123. Adult alder fly.

Bardogs Aldie (Donald Downs)

Fig. 124. Bardogs Aldie, tied by Donald Downs.

There are many more patterns of the adult alder fly than there are of the larva, which is odd because trout certainly see more larvae than they ever do winged adults. At a push, a mayfly nymph might do reasonably well, but this alder larva imitation, designed by APGAI instructor Donald Downs, does a much better job.

This fly uses a size 12 long-shank hook, cock-pheasant-tail fibres, a mixture of 25 per cent brown and 75 per cent natural wool (the latter from barbed wire fences!), fine silver wire rib, and latex adhesive.

To dress the Bardogs Aldie, cut a strip of pheasant-tail herls about 4 mm wide, level the points and cover them with latex adhesive for the last 10 mm – this will form the tail. Wind on a foundation layer of thread to the hook bend and tie in the rib and then the herl strip so that the tail projects over the hook bend. Dub the body material to 2 mm behind the eye, bring the herl strip over the dubbing and tie in. Rib in close turns to the head. To represent the gills, prick out material from between turns of the ribbing.

Fishing tip
Inch the Aldie along the bottom for a yard or so using a slow figure-of-eight retrieve and then pause for a few seconds. Takes are most likely to come just as you begin retrieving again.

Tadpole

(Rana temporaria, Bufo bufo)

Fig. 125. Tadpoles are mainly of interest to stillwater anglers.

Most stillwaters provide breeding habitat for the common frog and many of them are also used by toads. Frogs and toads start life as tadpoles wriggling in the margins in their thousands. Trout and other fishes thin out the hatch, as do herons and many other waterside creatures.

Frogs lay their spawn in large masses, while toads produce spawn in a continuous ribbon up to 12 ft in length entwined among water plants in the margins. The adults leave the water soon after spawning, but the tadpoles are available to trout for typically three months from April until June.

That trout eat tadpoles is indisputable. On occasion rainbow trout in particular can be seen attacking shoals of tadpoles all along the margins, and the only defence mechanism available to the tadpoles is to seek the shelter of marginal plants or the very shallow water where the fish would become stranded. It is not uncommon, however, to see brown trout cruising past tadpoles, and it may be that at such times they have either tired of the monotony of their diet or find them somewhat unpalatable.

Magnificent Seven: Coch-y-bonddu, size 12.

Marabou-tailed Tadpole

Fig. 126. Marabou-tailed Tadpole.

This is a very simple but effective fly for use when trout are feeding on tadpoles. The tail is a plume of black marabou, and the body is a peacock herl rope wound to form an oval hump. Depending upon the stage of development of the tadpoles, this fly may be tied on hooks of sizes 10 to 14.

A fly with no added weight is usually the most effective during warm weather; however, if the weather turns cold then a weighted version may be needed, as tadpoles tend to hug the bottom at such times. Copper wire or flat lead wire may be used as an underbody according to the weight required.

Fishing tip
Tadpoles rarely stray far from the relative safety of the margins, and so this fly is best fished along the banks rather than being cast out towards the middle of the lake.

A tadpole usually wriggles along for a short distance and then rests for a few moments before continuing in its search for food. This behaviour is easy to imitate with the Marabou-tailed Tadpole: simply give the line a few very short jerks, then wait a couple of seconds before retrieving once more. When using the weighted version of this fly, the takes often come 'on the drop', as the fly begins to settle towards the lake bed in between retrieves of line.

Chapter 5
Summer

The end of the mayfly hatch signals the beginning of the flyfisher's summer. There is no clear dividing line between the two seasons, but as the water temperature rises so the main fly hatches become confined to the cooler hours of morning and evening. It is still possible to catch trout during the day, but on lowland streams the nymph fisher is often far more successful than the dry-fly fisher, whose tactics work best early in the morning and in the evening rise.

The evening rise . . . now there is an enigma! Unless there is a strong wind, there are usually plenty of flies to be seen on and about the water during summer evenings, but the trout do not always appreciate the treat that Nature provides for them. There may be a frantic scrambling for food, a mad panic that lasts until the last drop of blood drains from the sky. There may be . . . but just as likely you will wait all evening and see or hear no more than the occasional desultory plop.

Fig. 127. A summer evening on the River Usk, with a cocktail of upwinged flies, sedges, stoneflies and midges in the air.

The flies of summer

Summer is a strange mixture. There are some very important upwinged flies, and it seems that some of them are not easy to copy (or maybe the trout get a clearer view in summer and can more easily detect the inadequacies in our imitations.)

Matching the upwinged fly hatch can be important in summer, particularly during the evening rise, and spinners can be as important as duns and sometimes more so.

The upwinged flies in this chapter fall into three main groups:

- Pale olive duns with golden or amber spinners.

- Medium-olive duns with predominantly orange spinners.

- Dark olive duns with predominantly brown spinners.

Increasing numbers of sedge flies are to be seen as summer takes over from spring. The larger sedges are evening flies, but there are also a few smaller species which are active from late morning onwards. Sedge larvae and pupae are important sources of sub-surface food on both river and stillwater.

There are probably only two summer stoneflies worthy of imitation, and they are the large and the small yellow sally. On some rough streams these are the only flies that trout have opportunities to rise for during bright sunny afternoons.

For the lake fisher, chironomid midges, or buzzers as they are commonly known, are undoubtedly the most significant source of trout food, and the pupae in particular are usually the cornerstone of the evening rise.

Summertime in the hills is delightful. While lowland waters are flat and silent, on hill lochs and mountain streams steady rises continue throughout the long summer days. There, terrestrial insects – beetles in particular – provide a variety of opportunities for matching the hatch.

Fig. 128. Summer trouting on a mountain stream, where terrestrial insects are the main source of food for the trout.

Pale watery

(Baëtis fuscatus)

Fig. 129. Pale watery dun (f).

In the past, several species of flies were called pale wateries. This group included the small spurwing, the large spurwing and the pale evening dun. For imitation purposes they can all be matched adequately with the same dun and spinner patterns, but to help those who have an interest in identifying individual species, illustrations of the other species are included on pages 118–122.

The pale watery dun

Today, when anglers talk about pale wateries they are usually referring to *Baëtis fuscatus*, a very common fly of rivers and streams in England, Wales and a few parts of Scotland. The nymphs are agile darters, and the duns hatch in open water from late morning until dusk. Hatches occur from June until the end of September.

Magnificent Seven: Tups Indispensable, size 16.

Fig. 130. Pale watery dun (m). The yellow eyes are a distinguishing feature of this fly.

Funneldun (Neil Patterson)

Fig. 131. Funneldun, tied by Neil Patterson.

Neil Patterson, that most inventive of flyfishers, devised this style of fly tying for fishing on an English chalk stream. The fly illustrated is an excellent general representation of the paler of the upwinged duns of summer – in particular, the pale watery, the small and large spurwing and the pale evening dun.

Neil Patterson ties this fly in sizes 14–18, on up-eyed hooks. The tying thread is chosen to match the hatch, and the head and a humpy dubbed thorax are tied first. The thorax material is light-coloured fluff from roots of mink pelt hairs, and the body is cream fur. A wing of grey mallard, widgeon or teal breast feathers may be added. The blue dun hackle is selected to match the hatch, and a few ginger cree cock hackle fibres make the tail, which is tied off with a whip finish.

A key feature of the Funneldun is the forward sloping hackle, which is funnelled out over the bulky thorax. A small V is cut from the underside of the hackle, and this ensures that the fly lands hook point in the air every time it is cast. Ingenious!

In addition to being a very effective copy of duns of the pale watery, the small and large spurwings and the pale evening dun, the Funneldun shown above will also serve as a representation of the medium olive, the pond and lake olives and the blue-winged olive, described later in this chapter.

The pale watery spinner

Fig. 132. Pale watery spinner (f).

In the evening, male spinners of the pale watery swarm along the edge of the river bank, and many end up on the surface. The female spinners fly low over the water until they find a partly submerged branch of a fallen tree, a bridge support etc, down which to crawl to lay their eggs beneath the water.

On returning to the surface, many female spinners become trapped either in or just beneath the surface film. It pays to fish your artificial spinner without floatant so as to mimic this aspect of the behaviour of the natural fly.

Brian Clarke's versatile Polythene-winged Spinner (page 117) is a good match for the spent pale watery spinner.

Magnificent Seven: Tups Indispensable, size 16.

Fig. 133. Pale watery spinner (m).

Polythene-winged Spinner (Brian Clarke)

Fig. 134. Polythene-winged Spinner, tied by Brian Clarke.

Together with John Goddard, Brian Clarke has given us *The Trout and The Fly*, one of the most successful books ever produced on the subject of trout fishing. Subsequently, via his angling and environment column in *The Times* and his own books on flyfishing, Brian has shared with many the insight he has gained from observing and fishing for trout throughout the world. One of the key points he stresses is that presentation is far more important than fly selection: a few good flies are all you need. Here is one of Brian Clarke's favourites.

The Polythene-winged Spinner uses a standard size 16 hook. The tail is of ginger cock hackle and the body requires an equal mix of olive and brown seal's fur (or substitute) with just a few fibres of hot orange added to the mixture. The body should be dubbed to leave a short space behind the eye; this is where the wing will go.

The wing material is polythene, cut from a clear kitchen bag. A long, narrow slip is fitted on top of the hook and secured with a figure-of-eight tying. This fly has no hackle.

When trout are taking spent spinners this fly, fished in or just under the surface film, is deadly. It is a particularly effective imitation of spinners of the river olives, the pale wateries and the spurwings.

Small spurwing

(Centroptilum luteolum)

Fig. 135. Small spurwing dun (f).

The small spurwing is mainly a river fly, although it is found in some lakes. The nymph is an agile darter and on chalk streams it is often found in large numbers among the weed beds. In rocky streams and upland lakes less prolific hatches of small spurwings occur.

The small spurwing dun

The tiny nymphs swim up to the surface when the duns are ready to emerge. Hatches occur throughout the summer and early autumn.

In the past this fly was known as the little sky-blue, owing to the colour of its wings, or simply classed as a pale watery; indeed, in Ireland where the pale watery, *Baëtis fuscatus*, is rarely if ever seen, the spurwings are still called pale wateries.

Magnificent Seven: Tups Indispensable, size 16 or 18.

Fig. 136. Small spurwing dun (m).

The small spurwing spinner

Fig. 137. Small spurwing spinner (f).

On June evenings, trout sometimes rise selectively to small spurwings, whereas later in the year there are more attractive morsels, such as blue-winged olive spinners, available. Both the male and the female spinners are important, because the males swarm along the margins and mating often takes place over the water. The female spinners lay their eggs by dipping down onto the water, and when spent they fall onto the surface where trout mop them up with gentle sipping rises as dusk descends.

Perhaps because it is so small, trout sometimes ignore this fly when larger spinners are available. A size 16 imitation then seems to work better than a more realistic size 18.

Magnificent Seven: Tups Indispensable, size 16 or 18.

Fig. 138. Small spurwing spinner (m).

Large spurwing

(Centroptilum pennulatum)

Fig. 139. Large spurwing dun (f).

This is a fly of lowland rivers and streams. When at rest it can usually be identified at a distance by not only its size (it is much larger than a pale watery or a small spurwing) but also its habit of resting with its wings set in a V rather than held closely together.

The large spurwing dun

The large spurwing nymph is an agile darter, and on spate rivers it appears to prefer fast-flowing water rather than the silty pools. In limestone rivers and chalk streams the nymphs are found among submerged weeds as well as tucked away under stones. From late May through to early autumn large spurwing duns come off open water with a steady, purposeful flight towards the treetops. Their numbers are generally too small to cause a selective rise.

Magnificent Seven: Tups Indispensable, size 14.

Fig. 140. Large spurwing dun (m).

The large spurwing spinner

Fig. 141. Large spurwing spinner (f).

Male spinners of the large spurwing swarm along the banks from late afternoon onwards and rarely get blown onto the surface in any numbers. The female spinners lay their eggs upon the surface, and spent spinners with outstretched wings drift on the current until the trout sip them down. Rises to spurwing spinners are leisurely affairs early in the evening, and the more splashy rises as darkness descends may simply be the result of trout seeing the flies at the last moment.

Falls of spinners are generally moderate, often coinciding with the availability of other, smaller flies. These are often the ingredients for a selective rise and so a reasonably close imitation, such as Brian Clarke's Polythene-winged Spinner, is called for.

Magnificent Seven: Tups Indispensable, size 14 or 16.

Fig. 142. Large spurwing spinner (m).

Pale evening

(Procloëon bifidum)

Fig. 143. Pale evening dun (f).

The pale evening dun is a fairly common fly on chalk streams and spate rivers, but as far as imitation is concerned, it is so similar to the dun of the pale watery that they can be treated as the same. Using an eyeglass, the two can be easily distinguished, however, because unlike the pale watery the pale evening dun does not have hindwings.

The nymph is another of the agile darters and has a preference for gentle glides and shallow pools rather than rapid water. In the evening, when the dun is ready to emerge, the nymph swims up to the surface. Pale evening spinners lay their eggs by touching down on the surface; they are occasionally blown onto the water before dark, but a specific imitation is hardly likely to be needed.

Magnificent Seven: Tups Indispensable, size 16.

Fig. 144. Pale evening spinner (m).

Duck's Dun (Charles Jardine)

Fig. 145. Duck's Dun, tied by Charles Jardine.

Charles Jardine, artist, author, broadcaster and angling instructor, needs no introduction. He has fished all around the globe and had plenty of opportunity to test his fly patterns on all kinds of waters. This is one of his favourite dun patterns.

The hook is a Partridge E6A, size 16, and a hot orange tying thread is used when copying the medium olive. The tails are fibres from the 'spade' hackle of a jungle cock (black and white), the body is dubbed from olive Hairtran, the colour being chosen to match the natural insect, and the wings are two cul-de-canard feathers, back-to-back, tied upright but sloping slightly back towards the hook bend. A very short blue dun hackle is added and clipped under and over, and then a whip-finished head completes the tying.

This version of the Duck's Dun is very effective when trout are taking the medium olive and the pond and lake olives, which are described on the following pages. To tailor the match to light olives such as the pale watery, the pale evening dun and the spurwings, use primrose tying thread and a paler body dubbing. Similarly, for darker flies such as the large dark olive switch to a claret tying thread and darker olive dubbing, and go up a hook size.

Medium olive

(Baëtis tenax, B. vernus)

Fig. 146. Medium olive dun (f).

The medium olive is one of the most important flies of early summer especially on chalk streams, where *Baëtis vernus* is the most widespread of the two species. *Baëtis tenax* occurs on both acid and alkaline streams and its hatches sometimes continue further into autumn. For both these species, hatches peak in May and June, and they usually continue to come off the water in fair numbers at least until August.

The medium olive dun

The agile darting nymph of the medium olive swims up to the surface when the dun is ready to emerge. Hatches usually begin in late morning and continue into the afternoon and early evening, with duns emerging in steady trickles rather than batches. Sometimes the resulting fall of spinners can be dense enough to cause a selective evening rise.

Apart from being slightly smaller than its future mate, the male dun of the medium olive is very similar to the female and has the same grey wings. Its body is often somewhat greyer, and it has large, ruddy-brown eyes.

Magnificent Seven: Greenwell's Glory, size 16.

The medium olive spinner

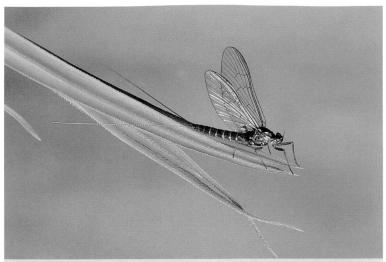

Fig. 147. Medium olive spinner (f).

Male spinners of the medium olive swarm along the banks of the river from mid-afternoon until dusk, and their dancing flight is extremely energetic. Female spinners may be seen flying low above the surface: in common with other *Baëtis* flies, they will be looking for objects protruding from the water so that they can crawl down them to lay their eggs under the water.

Both wind-borne male spinners and spent female spinners can give the trout cause to rise towards the end of the evening. Of the two, the females are the more important, and an imitation fished awash in, or even just beneath, the surface film will usually give better results than a fly floating high upon the surface.

Magnificent Seven: Tups Indispensable, size 16.

Fig. 148. Medium olive spinner (m).

Small dark olive

(Baëtis scambus)

Fig. 149. Small dark olive dun (f).

This tiny upwinged fly is found on all sorts of rivers and streams but is particularly abundant on fast-flowing chalk streams.

The small dark olive dun

The nymph, an agile darter which spends most of its time under stones or among streamer weeds and marginal plants, swims up to the surface when the dun is ready to emerge. The main hatch is in late summer and early autumn, but, as with other members of the *Baëtis* genus, small numbers can be seen throughout spring, summer and autumn.

Flies which closely match the medium olive will do very well for this fly, too. Ideally they need to be at least one size smaller.

Magnificent Seven: Greenwell's Glory, size 18.

Fig. 150. Small dark olive dun (m).

The small dark olive spinner

Fig. 151. Small dark olive spinner (f).

Male spinners swarm beneath bankside trees and only a small proportion end up on the water; however, on very breezy afternoons they can cause brief flurries of surface activity. The female spinners are much more important, however.

The female spinner, like the spinners of other *Baëtis* flies, lays her eggs after crawling down beneath the surface. From late afternoon until dark, spent small dark olive spinners can be seen drifting downstream trapped beneath the surface film, and in July and August they offer the trout good reason to celebrate with a feast. Rises are usually leisurely, as fish lie just beneath the surface and sip down these small red spinners with a minimum of effort.

Magnificent Seven: Tups Indispensable, size 18.

Fig. 152. Evening fishing, when trout rise to small dark olive spinners trapped beneath the surface film.

Lake olive

(Cloëon simile)

Fig. 153. Lake olive dun (f).

The lake olive is found in large lakes where the water temperature is relatively steady compared with that in the small ponds where the pond olive, its closest relative, is more commonly found. The two species are quite similar, but the duller lake olive has grey tails whereas those of the pond olive are clearly ringed with brown.

The lake olive dun

The nymph is an agile darter, and the dun leaves the surface in open water, often some distance from the shore. The main hatches occur from late morning onwards in early summer and again in late summer and early autumn, and can be prolific. Lake olive duns vary greatly in size and colour, larger individuals often being darker. The autumn lake olives are usually smaller than those of early summer.

Magnificent Seven: Greenwell's Glory, sizes 12 to 16.

Fig. 154. Lake olive dun (m).

Lake Olive (Peter Masters)

Fig. 155. Lake Olive, tied by Peter Masters.

The lake olive is such an important fly to reservoir anglers that it deserves a close imitation, even though it is most unlikely that the trout will see any other upwinged fly on the water in significant numbers at a time when lake olives are hatching. If the fish are at all fussy, here is a pattern which they are unlikely to reject.

This Lake Olive was devised by Peter Masters, who fishes the rich limestone waters of the Langford fishery. There the trout see large hatches of buzzers and of lake olives, and in the margins fish fry and *Corixae* (lesser water boatmen) are also plentiful.

Peter's Lake Olive is tied on a size 14 hook. The tail is a few hairs from a fine artist's paint brush, and the sparsely dubbed abdomen and thorax are of light olive Antron applied using a dubbing loop. The abdomen only is ribbed with fine silver wire. This is another fly which takes advantage of modern plastics: the wings are punched from a pale green plastic bag. Finally a cul-de-canard hackle and a whip-finished head complete the fly.

Although intended as a lake olive imitation, this fly also doubles as a pond olive, which means that one pattern will do for both of the olive flies most commonly encountered on stillwaters.

The lake olive spinner

Fig. 156. Lake olive spinner (f).

Lake olive spinners lay their eggs by dipping down to the surface of the water during the afternoon and evening and into the hours of darkness. Sometimes the fall of lake olive spinners is sufficient to cause a selective evening rise, and then a Lunn's Particular (page 131) can be an effective fly.

Male spinners of the lake olive swarm around the edges of lakes and reservoirs, and if there are trees some distance from the water's edge the male spinners tend to congregate beneath them and are unlikely to fall onto the water in any numbers unless the wind is blustery; a Pheasant Tail Spinner (page 83) is then a useful fly. Otherwise, it is as well to concentrate on imitating the female spinner, and particularly in its spent form.

Magnificent Seven: Tups Indispensable, size 14.

Fig. 157. Lake olive spinner (m).

Lunn's Particular (William Lunn)

Fig. 158. Lunn's Particular, tied in 1964 by Albert Lunn.

For generations, the Lunn family have keepered the Houghton Club's waters of the River Test near Stockbridge, in Hampshire. There, in 1917, William Lunn revealed this fly to the flyfishing world. It was intended primarily as an imitation of the medium olive spinner. Not only has Lunn's Particular remained a firm favourite on the chalk streams of southern England, but it has also been adopted by dry-fly fishers on spate rivers throughout the world. As well as following in his father's footsteps as a river keeper, Albert Lunn tied flies professionally. In 1964 he tied the Lunn's Particular illustrated here.

Because the medium olive is a fly which varies greatly in size from one specimen to another, it is useful to have its imitation tied on more than one size of hook. Sizes 14 and 16 are most useful.

The tail is of pale buff cock hackle fibres, the body is wound from white hackle stalk dyed yellow, and the wings are made with light buff cock hackle fibre tied in the spent position.

As well as being a close copy of the medium olive, Lunn's Particular was recommended by its originator as a good representation of the spinner of the large dark olive (a lesser role, admittedly, since only rarely are trout seen rising to large dark olive spinners).

Pond olive

(Cloëon dipterum)

Fig. 159. Pond olive dun (f).

For those who fish on small stillwaters the pond olive is the most important of the upwinged flies. Pond olive nymphs are agile darters, varying greatly in colour: some are mainly brown while others remain medium olive right up to the point of hatching.

The pond olive dun

Pond olive duns are equally variable in colour when they first hatch, but all tend to darken with age. The duns, which appear from late morning through until early evening, come off the surface in open water. Hatches are usually greatest in June and again in September, but even in high summer small numbers of pond olives can be expected. Like lake olives, they vary considerably in size.

Magnificent Seven: Greenwell's Glory, size 14 or 16.

Fig. 160. Pond olive dun (m).

The pond olive spinner

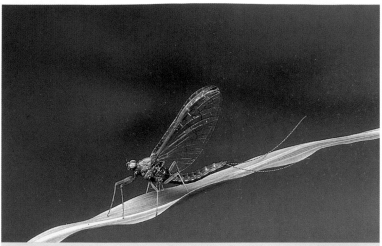

Fig. 161. Pond olive spinner (f).

The pond olive spinner is viviparous, which means that the eggs hatch inside the body of the adult and swim away as soon as they are released onto the surface. Unusual in behaviour and striking in appearance as it is, the pond olive spinner is rarely as important as the dun because it has a habit of releasing its young after nightfall. Trout are sometimes seen sipping the spent spinners from the margins early in the morning, when a suitable imitation can prove effective.

Male spinners swarm around the edges of the water, and on blustery evenings it is always possible that some will end up in the water; however, as they tend to swarm well above the ground it takes quite a gust to deposit these adept flyers in the drink. If you need a reasonably close copy of the male spinner, try a Houghton Ruby.

Magnificent Seven: Tups Indispensable, size 14.

Fig. 162. Pond olive spinner (m).

Blue-winged olive

(Ephemerella ignita)

Fig. 163. The River Test, where the b-w o is one of the most important flies of late spring and summer.

If you fish on rivers, you will certainly come across good hatches of this medium-sized fly. The adult is easily recognised: it is bigger than most other upwinged flies of summer and it is one of the select few that retain all three tails. On chalk streams the nymph of the b-w o, as this fly is colloquially termed, inhabits the submerged weed beds and the mosses around bridge pilings. The female spinner is nearly always a major contributor to the evening rise as she returns to the river with a ball of green eggs tucked beneath her abdomen and deposits them on the surface.

On many chalk streams there is a hatch of blue-winged olives all through the year, although the hatches are greatest between June and September, during which time they are also to be seen on most lowland rough streams and on quite a few hill streams, too.

The b-w o is not often encountered on small stillwaters unless there is a good through flow. Fishing near the inlet and outlet streams is often a wise move if you do see b-w o duns in the air. These adaptable upwinged flies do also occur in reasonable numbers on some of the larger stillwaters where there is sufficient wave action to create the current they need.

The b-w o nymph
(a typical moss creeper)

Fig. 164. The b-w o nymph.

This slightly flattened nymph is less streamlined than the agile darters. It has a domed thorax and abdomen, almost black on top with a lighter underside, and strong legs. In fast-flowing, rain-fed rough streams, b-w o nymphs spend most of their time under the stones, where they are able to graze in relative safety upon algae and mosses. Here, too, they often make an important contribution to summer flyfishing.

This nymph is a moss creeper, and so on stony streams it barely features on the trout's menu except during a hatch. In limestone rivers and chalk streams the fish forage among the streamer weeds to dislodge these nymphs, which 'freeze' when disturbed and so become easy pickings.

On bright days trout seem to find it easier to intercept b-w o nymphs as they swim up towards the surface, rather than dashing to catch the new-born duns as they skitter before taking off from the water. There are many artificial flies which represent this emerging dun stage, but the simple Gold-ribbed Hare's Ear (page 47) is probably one of the most effective. It should, of course, be tied without a weighted underbody. Try fishing it just beneath the surface by greasing all but the last three inches of your leader.

Magnificent Seven: GRHE, size 14.

The b-w o dun

Fig. 165. B-w o dun (f).

The main summer hatch, which can be particularly dense on heavily weeded streams, begins in the late afternoon or early evening and often continues until dark. It is common for duns and spinners to be on the water at the same time, contributing to a frenetic evening rise. The challenge then is to find out which stage of the life-cycle the trout are showing preference for – nymphs just below the surface, duns on the surface, egg-laying spinners as they touch down, or spent spinners as they lie prostrate in the surface film.

The dun emerges from its nymphal skin at the surface in open water, and on humid days it may require two or three attempts before it becomes airborne. During these flight trials the new-born fly is extremely vulnerable to surface-feeding trout.

Magnificent Seven: Greenwell's Glory, size 14.

Fig. 166. B-w o dun (m).

Clonanav CDC Dun (Andrew Ryan)

Fig. 167. Clonanav CDC Dun, tied by Andrew Ryan.

Certain parts of a duck really do have to be watertight, and the feathers from that region are also superlative in their resistance to waterlogging. Cul-de-canard feathers from the oil glands of a duck's posterior first found their way into fly tying on the continent of Europe, but they are now firmly established world wide.

Andrew Ryan of Clonanav Angling Centre, near Clonmel, developed this dun for the turbulent waters of the River Suir and its tributaries. The tail consists of three Coq-de-Leon fibres, the body uses olive Fly-Rite dubbing, and the wings are cul-de-canard tied in wonderwing style. Cul-de-canard is also used to represent the legs.

As a b-w o dun imitation it is a great pattern, but it also works pretty well when trout are taking light or medium *Baëtis* olives.

Fishing tips
Because duns rarely fall from the sky, except on very windy days, a fly dropped close to a trout may arouse its suspicions; if so, cast further upstream and allow your CDC Dun to drift into the trout's window. (Drifting duns have little control of direction, and, while a small amount of surface skating is characteristic of a struggling fly, it is important to avoid excessive drag.)

The b-w o spinner

Fig. 168. B-w o spinner (f) with her egg ball.

The female spinner is a most important late-afternoon and evening fly during the summer months. Some writers have suggested that trout prefer these flies to any others which might be on the water at the same time. I doubt that: trout generally swallow small insects whole, and so the question of flavour is unlikely to matter. This apparent preference is probably due to the behaviour *and* to the colour of the spent spinner: dead flies do not have the annoying habit of flying off just before a hungry trout reaches the surface; and the body of the spent female b-w o spinner is orange (it is commonly referred to as the sherry spinner) and viewed from beneath the surface it is highly visible in the ruddy glow of a warm summer's evening.

Magnificent Seven: Tups Indispensable, size 14.

Fig. 169. B-w o spinner (m).

Sherry Spinner (William Lunn)

Fig. 170. Sherry Spinner, tied by Alice Conba

This very useful late-evening pattern is the invention of William Lunn. It uses bright orange body material which shows up well in the orange light of a fine summer evening. The hook is size 14, the tail of light ginger cock fibres, and the deep orange floss body is ribbed with gold wire. Pale blue dun hackle points are used for the spent wings, and a hackle of Rhode Island Red cock completes the tying.

Alice Conba's adaptation of Lunn's design uses orange seal's fur as the body dubbing and Antron for the wings.

This version of the Sherry Spinner is most successful during an evening rise to b-w o spinners. It is also a pretty effective imitation of the spurwing and pale watery spinners.

Fishing tips
Unlike duns, spinners *do* drop in from the sky, and so a Sherry Spinner cast close to a rising trout should not arouse its suspicions. If you give the fish very little time to inspect your offering, it has to make a snap decision without scrutinising your fly closely. When fishing the spent spinner, drag is the enemy. Dead flies remain inert; flies attached to leaders rarely drift very far without dragging and creating a wake.

Large green dun and spinner

(Ecdyonurus insignis)

Fig. 171. Large green dun (f).

The large green dun is a river fly, and its nymph is a stone clinger. It is normally seen only in small numbers, mainly on spate rivers with stony beds. The nymph generally crawls out of the water when the dun is ready to emerge, and so only rarely are duns available to the trout. Male and female duns are very similar in appearance.

The spinner has distinctive dark patches on the leading edges of the forewings. Male and female spinners are similar except that the tails of the male are unusually long. Paired spinners are often seen flying upstream not far from the surface, but there are usually too few of them to cause a selective rise.

Magnificent Seven: Greenwell's Glory, size 12.

Fig. 172. Large green spinner (m). Note the remarkably long tails.

Ecdyonurid Spinner (Malcolm Greenhalgh)

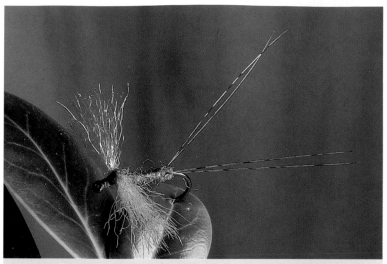

Fig. 173. Ecdyonurid Spinner, tied by Malcolm Greenhalgh.

Malcolm Greenhalgh is well known for his books, articles and broadcasts on flyfishing. He is particularly familiar with the spate rivers of the north of England where there are at times very good hatches of ecdyonurids and, consequently, falls of spent flies such as the spinner of the large green dun.

The tying of the Ecdyonurid Spinner is quite straightforward. Malcolm uses a size 12 Partridge L3A hook for imitating the larger spinners. The tail is of brown cock hackle fibres (or Coq-de-Leon), the body is rusty orange Antron, and the wing is white or light blue dun Antron, tied spent.

This is a spent spinner pattern devised for the rough streams and the spate rivers. As well as providing a close imitation of the large green spinner, this fly is also useful when false march brown spinners are on the water in late spring and early summer (when it is best tied on a size 14 hook), and when you need an imitation of the large red spinner of the autumn dun.

The Ecdyonurid Spinner can also be useful when trout are taking spent spinners of the large brook dun (page 76), and it might be worth trying as a dusky yellowstreak spinner (page 143).

Dusky yellowstreak

(*Heptagenia lateralis*)

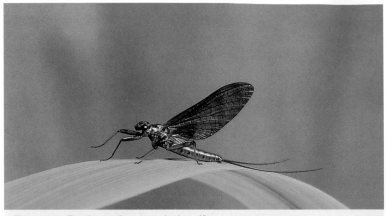

Fig. 174. Dusky yellowstreak dun (f).

Bright yellow streaks on the thorax just below the wing roots give this summer fly its common name. (It used to be called the dark dun, as it still is in some areas.) The nymph, another of the stone clingers, is very common on spate rivers and also occurs on some upland lakes, particularly those where the shores are exposed to strong winds which create wave action along the stony shores.

The dusky yellowstreak dun

The dusky yellowstreak dun emerges from its nymphal skin beneath the water and swims up to the surface. It is the only dun in the British Isles which behaves in this way. Hatches, which occur during late afternoon throughout the summer months, are rarely dense and close imitation is not generally necessary.

Magnificent Seven: Greenwell's Glory, size 14.

Fig. 175. Dusky yellowstreak dun (m).

The dusky yellowstreak spinner

Fig. 176. Dusky yellowstreak spinner (f).

Male spinners swarm in relatively small groups, often some distance from the water, and are unlikely to be worth close imitation – in any case the colour difference between the sexes of this fly is not great.

The female spinners are more important than the males, as they lay their eggs by dipping their abdomens into the surface before taking off and flying a short distance, whereupon the process is repeated. On occasions I have seen trout rising to the spent spinners of the dusky yellowstreak, but at such times they have not proved particularly selective in their feeding and appeared to be taking other, smaller flies with equal enthusiasm. A Pheasant Tail Spinner (page 83) should be a good choice if you do need a close copy.

Magnificent Seven: Greenwell's Glory, size 14.

Fig. 177. Dusky yellowstreak spinner (m).

The purple dun

(Paraleptophlebia cincta)

Fig. 178. Purple dun (f).

This fly of fast, stony streams is found both on lowland rivers and high up in the hills. Its nymph, one of the smaller members of the laboured swimmers group, spends most of its life among the sparse mosses which grow between stones and marginal plants.

Purple duns emerge at the surface from mid-morning until late afternoon. Male spinners swarm from midday onwards, generally over the water, and they are similar to iron blue spinners except for their three tails (the iron blue has only two). The females lay their eggs around or after dusk. On the few rivers where a close copy is justified, iron blue dun and spinner imitations are well worth a try.

Magnificent Seven: Greenwell's Glory, size 16.

Fig. 179. Purple spinner (m).

Caënis

(Caënis and *Brachycercus* species*)*

Fig. 180. A *Caënis* dun (f).

Five *Caënis* species and one *Brachycercus* species are found in the British Isles. The nymphs live in the shallows of lakes and in the silty backwaters of lowland rivers and streams, where they feed among the debris on the bottom. Caënis are often present in vast numbers, and when trout lock onto the duns or the spinners it is almost pointless continuing to fish. Why should a trout take your offering in preference to the many hundreds of others available at the same time?

The caënis dun

These tiny flies, mostly no more than 4 mm long, have for years been known as the anglers' curse or the white curse.

Very pale caënis duns hatch in the evening on lakes, while on rivers there is often a morning hatch of somewhat greyer duns, too.

Magnificent Seven: No effective imitation.

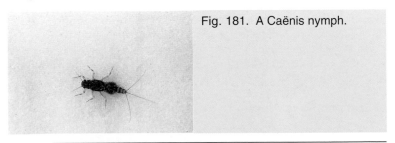

Fig. 181. A Caënis nymph.

The caënis spinner

Fig. 182. Caënis spinner (m).

There are times when trout selectively take caënis flies even though there are larger spent spinners on the water. On an evening when the trout are feeding exclusively on spent caënis, the chances of success depend greatly on just how heavy the hatch has been, and the rise form may be a clue to this. The rise is often a very leisurely affair when the fall of spinners is only moderate, but in a really dense fall the trout sometimes make vigorous head-and-tail rises and they may well be taking groups of caënis rather than singletons.

The transformation from dun to spinner occurs as soon as the dun alights after leaving the surface of the water. Anglers are able to watch this miracle of nature time after time as scores of duns land on their clothing and immediately turn into spinners. Within a minute or two the spinner is back in the air and is soon ready to mate. (Caënis duns also settle on waders, sunglasses, car roofs, etc, and their attempts to transpose into spinners on these non-porous surfaces are often unsuccessful; anglers are left to clean up afterwards!)

Both the male and the female spinner are similar in appearance to the duns, but one remarkable feature of the male spinner is the length of its tails, which can be more than three times the body length.

Magnificent Seven: No effective imitation.

Conba Caënis

Fig. 183. Caënis Flies, tied by Alice Conba.

Provided the hatch is not excessively dense, and this is often the case on rivers in the morning, a slightly larger than life imitation will sometimes bring the downfall of a trout that is feeding exclusively on caënis. (To use this tactic, you may need to get out onto the river an hour or more before breakfast in mid-summer, because caënis are early risers!)

Alice Conba, an internationally renowned fly tyer who works from a studio in Cahir on Ireland's famous River Suir, ties her Caënis Flies in an all-white strip. They work very well as imitations of both the greyish duns and the creamy-white spinners. The body is white tying thread, the tails and the hackle are white cock, and the wing, when required, is white cul-de-canard. Those in the illustration are tied on size 22 hooks.

Fishing tip
If the hatch is extremely dense, as evening hatches in particular can be, a contrasting fly usually provides the best chance of taking a fish or two. I have had some success with a size 14 Silver Sedge on rich limestone rivers in the evenings when trout have locked onto spent caënis spinners – even when there were blue-winged olives, spurwings and small dark olives available at the same time!

The large summer dun

(Siphlonurus lacustris)

Fig. 184. Large summer dun (f).

This very large fly is found in lakes and slow-flowing rivers. Many of the Scottish lochs and the limestone loughs of Ireland have moderate populations of large summer duns, but the trickle hatches, which occur mainly in June, July and August, are rarely prolific.

The nymph is an agile darter, and is reputed to crawl into the shallows and onto emergent vegetation or exposed rocks when the dun is ready to emerge. Large summer duns are normally to be seen near the margins in the afternoons. Later, male spinners generally swarm over the water quite close to the shore, and, after mating, the females lay their eggs by touching down onto the surface. The sexes are very similar in appearance at both the dun and the spinner stages.

Magnificent Seven: Greenwell's Glory, size 10.

Fig. 185. Large summer spinner (f).

Welshman's button

(Sericostoma personatum)

Fig. 186. Welshman's button.

Despite its name, which it was given by F M Halford, the father of dry-fly fishing, this sedge fly is as much at home on the chalk streams of Hampshire as it is in the Welsh valleys. It is confined to flowing water, and has a preference for the faster rivers and streams.

Hatches mainly occur in the afternoons and often there is such an abundance of these sedge flies as to cause quite a stir in the trout world. During a hatch, fishing with an emerging sedge pupa (page 153) is often more fruitful than using a dry fly.

These sedge flies are usually to be seen throughout the summer months and into early autumn.

Magnificent Seven: Silver Sedge, size 14.

Fig. 187. A sand-based larval case of the type built by the Welshman's button. A case with some weight is essential in fast-flowing streams.

Large cinnamon sedge

(Potamophylax latipennis)

Fig. 188. A large cinnamon sedge.

A very important fly of summer and early autumn is the large cinnamon sedge. It is essentially a river fly, and is seen mainly as dusk approaches. The main hatching period is from late July until the middle of September, but occasional specimens can sometimes be found as early as June and as late as the end of October. It is sometimes confused with the caperer (page 186), a rather duller sedge fly of similar size.

As with many of the sedges, this fly shares its common name with several other species of similar size and colouring. A green-bodied G&H Sedge (page 155) is an ideal imitative pattern, because the body of the large cinnamon sedge is often an olive green colour.

Magnificent Seven: Silver Sedge, size 12.

Fig. 189. A sedge larva in its case built from small pebbles. This type of case is favoured by the large cinnamon sedge.

Rubbery Caddis

Fig. 190. Rubbery Caddis.

In common with many other caddis grubs, the larva of the large cinnamon sedge uses small pebbles to construct its mobile home, and there is no doubt that when the larva is stationary it is superbly camouflaged. But once the larva begins trundling about in search of food, its lifestyle takes on an element of risk: large trout will not hesitate to swallow this type of cased caddis, house and all.

Richard Walker devised a cased caddis imitation made by gluing sand and small pebbles to the shank of a hook. It looked realistic, but lacked the 'squidginess' of the real thing. I have found that quite frequently a trout will rapidly eject a solid fly but will hang on longer to a soft-bodied one; the Rubbery Caddis is a cure for this problem.

The body is made from an elastic band wound on a size 12 long-shank hook and tied in place with a whip finish and a brown head hackle. The rubber is coated with glue – a flexible adhesive such as Bostik is preferable to one that sets hard – and then grit is sprinkled over the body. This gives a durable but flexible caddis.

You can, of course, use many other body materials, including small snail shells and bits of stick, to match the architectural preferences of the various caddis grubs you find most common on each fishery. And on weedy waters, it helps if you tie the hackle at the hook bend to act as a weed guard; you should then have no difficulty catching backward trout!

Cinnamon sedge

(Limnephilus lunatus)

Fig. 191. A cinnamon sedge.

The cinnamon sedge is found on rivers, lakes and some small still-waters. It is on the wing throughout summer and early autumn and can be seen flying from early afternoon until dusk. Hatches are moderate to good, but like other large sedges this fly does not tend to swarm. The body of *Limnephilus lunatus* is green, and a very effective imitation is the G&H Sedge (page 155) tied with a pinch of green seal's fur or Antron beneath its body.

Many sedge flies of similar shape and general colouring, but not bearing lunar markings on the wings, have been given the common name of cinnamon sedge. Trout do not appear to differentiate closely between these and other moderately large sedge flies.

Magnificent Seven: Silver Sedge, size 14.

Fig. 192. This sedge pupa is ready to hatch. Trout sometimes select the rising pupa of the cinnamon sedge in preference to the newly emerged adult.

Caddis Pupa (Davy Wotton)

Fig. 193. Caddis Pupa, tied by Davy Wotton.

Although there is no doubt that trout eat sedges at their larva and adult stages, at no time is the sedge fly more vulnerable than when the pupa emerges from its case and begins rising to the surface. It is probable that most trout eat many more sedge pupae than they do adult sedge flies, and yet fly dressers down the ages have tended to concentrate on the adults.

One of the first really successful sedge pupa patterns, the Amber Nymph, was devised by Dr Howard Bell, who fished on the Bristol reservoirs in the 1920s and 30s. Davy Wotton has developed Bell's concept to a fine art with this SLF-based design, complete with antennae swept back over the body. Davy suggests that legs may be added if you so wish, although the fly seems to work perfectly well without them.

Size 6/0 white tying thread is recommended. The hook is Partridge GRS12ST, K2B or CS27 (barbless); the body is a dubbed SLF (numbers 5, 7, 10, 16, 20, 37 and 48 are well suited to caddis pupa imitation) applied using the 'split thread' technique; and the wing is Raffene, trimmed to a curve and tied in so that it rolls around the body. A hen hackle, a traditionally dubbed head and a pair of bronze mallard or wood duck fibre antennae complete the tying. If you want to include legs, a partridge hackle is ideal for this purpose.

Great red sedge

(Phrygania grandis, P. striata)

Fig. 194. Great red sedge, *Phrygania striata.*

This is the largest sedge fly that hatches in British waters. At typically 25 mm from head to wing tip, it presents a trout with quite as big a mouthful as a mayfly. When on the surface of the water, the body of a sedge is visible to a trout approaching from below. The body of *P. grandis* is grey, while that of *P. striata* is greenish-grey. In Ireland *P. grandis* is known as the murragh, and it is a very important fly on the great limestone lakes.

These are flies of the lakes and the slow-flowing rivers. The great red sedges hatch in late afternoon and early evening. First appearing towards the end of May, they are normally to be seen in fair numbers through June and into July, with occasional specimens about through to mid-August.

The larva makes its case from plant material which it fashions into a spiral form. As the young larva develops it attaches more material to the larger (head) end of the case. After a pupation phase, the adult sedge fly emerges at the surface and heads for land, often skittering across the water for some distance. Great red sedges often settle within crevices in the weathered limestone, where they are less vulnerable to predation by birds.

Magnificent Seven: Silver Sedge, size 12.

G&H Sedge (John Goddard and Cliff Henry)

Fig. 195. G&H Sedge.

John Goddard and Cliff Henry devised this very useful fly, which has attained great popularity on stillwaters. It is also a very useful river pattern when trout are taking large sedge flies, such as the cinnamon sedge, in the evenings. Hook sizes 8 to 12 are most useful.

The tying involves spinning bunches of deer hair close together along the hook shank and then clipping the deer hair to a sedge fly shape. A twist of either green or orange seal's fur or Antron is tied in beneath the hook and carried forward to just behind the eye of the hook, where it is tied down; this represents the body of the sedge. (Use green body material when copying the great red sedge.) Two rusty dun cock hackles are wound on at the head, and their hackle stalks are used to represent the antennae of the insect. As an alternative, a pair of badger fibres will perform this function and they are more flexible than the hackle stalks. A whip-finished head completes the fly.

Fishing tip
After sunset, try a G&H Sedge twitched very occasionally, or even skittered along beside reed beds where sedge flies are likely to hatch. Takes can be particularly vicious, as this tactic will often rise large trout which would not exert themselves for mere upwinged flies.

Brown silverhorn sedge

(Anthripsodes species*)*

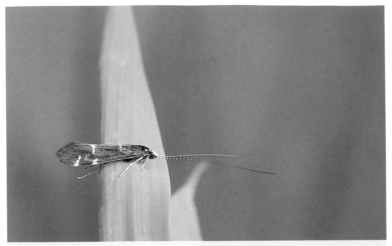

Fig. 196. Brown silverhorn sedge, *Anthripsodes albifrons.*

Brown silverhorn sedge flies are very common and widespread, and they hatch in large numbers. Brown silverhorns have long antennae and dark brown or sometimes black bodies. They appear throughout the summer months on rivers and on lakes, and swarms are usually seen from late afternoon onwards.

On rivers, these energetic little sedges swirl just above the surface in shady places (beneath sycamore trees seems to be a particularly popular meeting place for silverhorns), and occasionally trout can be seen leaping at them, perhaps in the hope of knocking one or two onto the surface. A suitable dry fly cast gently through the swarm, so as not to disperse them, is a very successful tactic at such times.

Magnificent Seven: Silver Sedge, size 14.

Fig. 197. Brown silverhorns swarm beneath the trees on summer evenings.

Deveaux Sedge (Aimé Deveaux)

Fig. 198. Deveaux Sedge, tied by Andrew Ryan.

When natural sedge flies are sitting high upon the surface there is a host of artificial patterns to choose from, but when the egg-laying sedges are spent and settle into the surface the Deveaux style of tying reigns supreme.

The body colour can be represented by a sparse dubbing – in the case of the brown silverhorns this should be dark grey-brown, and SLF is an ideal material for this purpose. Mallard breast feathers are used for the wings, one feather being tied on each side of the hook and a third feather over the top. A brown cock hackle and then a whip-finished head are added to complete the fly. The most useful hook size is 14 long shank.

For evening fishing the body material is an unnecessary luxury, and the Deveaux Sedge may be tied with only the wings and the hackle. What could be simpler?

When trout are taking summer sedges swamped in the surface film, the colours of the artificial fly seem to be of little importance. The size 14 Deveaux Sedge illustrated here will also serve as a copy of other darkish sedges of medium size, but it is a simple matter to alter the hook size to suit any particularly large or small sedge flies seen upon the water; sizes 12 to 16 should cover most requirements.

Marbled sedge

(Hydropsyche contubernalis)

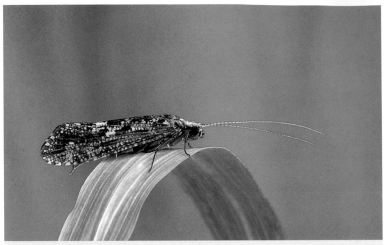

Fig. 199. A marbled sedge.

This medium-sized sedge is essentially a river fly. Its larva builds a case from small pebbles and sand particles and constructs a net at one end of the case in order to catch its food. The larva of the marbled sedge is mainly found in moderately fast water. On lakes, it is normally restricted to stony or gravelly areas in the vicinity of inflowing streams.

The adults, which have green bodies, hatch throughout the summer months. They are often seen during the afternoon and evening swirling in small groups along the banks and beneath marginal trees, and like so many of the summer sedge flies they seem to have a preference for shady places.

Magnificent Seven: Silver Sedge, size 14.

Fig. 200. Tree-lined rivers provide ideal habitat for the marbled sedge.

Grouse wing sedge

(Mystacides longicornis)

Fig. 201. A grouse wing sedge.

This fly gets its common name from the distinctive markings on its wings, which are banded like the wing feathers of a grouse. The grouse wing sedges are found in abundance on stillwaters throughout the British Isles, and in settled weather extremely dense hatches occur on some large lakes, lochs and loughs. The bodies of these little sedges are generally dark brown.

Grouse wing sedges hatch in the afternoon and spend the heat of the day in low bushes and other vegetation around the margins. They are seen on the wing in the evening throughout summer and into early autumn.

Magnificent Seven: Silver Sedge, size 14.

Fig. 202. The grouse wing sedge hatches can be extremely dense on some large stillwaters.

Yellow sally

(*Isoperla grammatica*)

Fig. 203. The yellow sally.

This stonefly, sometimes called the large yellow sally, is one of the few flies which you are likely to see about in the midday sun during high summer. In some areas it is as common in spring as it is in summer, but elsewhere the hatches remain very sparse until late June.

The yellow sally is mainly a river fly, and it occurs in all sorts of lowland waterways. Largest concentrations are generally found on stony or gravelly spate rivers, where the yellow sally nymph seems to prefer moderately fast water up to 3 ft deep. As with other stoneflies, this nymph crawls out of the water before the winged adult emerges, and so it is the egg-laying female which provides the best opportunity for imitative flyfishing.

Magnificent Seven: Tups Indispensable, size 12.

Fig. 204. Yellow sally stoneflies are often seen in summer on small stony streams with plenty of tree cover.

Small yellow sally

(Chloroperla torrentium)

Fig. 205. Small yellow sally.

This common little stonefly occurs on rivers and large lakes. Females are often seen during the day flying upriver at head height before descending to the surface to release their eggs.

The first adults usually appear in May, but reasonable hatches continue through summer and into early autumn. On rivers the nymphs are found among weeds and under stones, while on lakes they are generally restricted to wind-swept margins where waves wash against stony shores. The nymphs usually crawl out of the water when the adults are ready to emerge, although I have on many occasions found winged flies beneath submerged stones in fast-flowing shallow water.

Magnificent Seven: Tups Indispensable, size 14.

Fig. 206. A small yellow sally nymph.

Summer midge

(*Chironomus* species)

Fig. 207. A chironomid larva, or bloodworm.

The summer midge larva

The larvae of chironomid midges are commonly called bloodworms, although not all of them are red. The red coloration comes from haemoglobin in the blood of the larva, and this enables it to live in water with a relatively low oxygen content.

Many species of chironomid larvae live in tubes made from silt, and the only fishes likely to feed upon them at this stage are mud-sifters such as the grayling and the coarse fishes. These larvae do sometimes leave their tubular homes, and there are also some species which move freely about the bottom and are potential food sources for trout.

Magnificent Seven: No effective imitation.

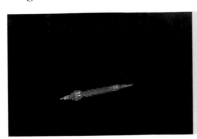

Fig. 208. The transparent phantom midge larva, *Chaoborus* species, is hardly worth trying to imitate with an artificial fly (trout would see through the deception!).

Bloodworm (John Wilshaw)

Fig. 209. Bloodworm, tied by John Wilshaw.

Author, journalist and former editor of *Trout and Salmon*, John Wilshaw devised this simple but very effective bloodworm imitation; it has become a standard pattern for stillwater fishing when trout are feeding in deep water. Tied in smaller sizes, Wilshaw's Bloodworm could find application on deep, slow-flowing rivers too.

This is one of the simplest of all fishing flies to tie. The hook is a size 12 or 14, and the tying thread is black. For the body dubbing, red seal's fur is used. The body, which should extend part-way round the hook bend, is ribbed with fine red copper wire. A whip finish at the head completes the fly.

Fishing tip
The Bloodworm should be fished deep and retrieved very slowly, or close to the surface (and a little faster) late on hot summer evenings.

Fig. 210. This 2 lb brown trout had been feeding on bloodworms as well as buzzer pupae.

The summer midge pupa

Fig. 211. An olive buzzer pupa.

The pupae of the summer midges range through most of the colour spectrum including deep red, brown, fawn, light olive, dark olive and black. Most of the summer species prepare for emergence in the late afternoon and evening, and that is when a team of buzzer pupa imitations can be most effective.

The discarded shucks from buzzers which have hatched also provide a valuable source of food for trout – around 25 per cent of the protein of a small insect is contained in its outer skin – and, of course, they do not fly away. Trout take them from the surface with leisurely, sipping rises.

Magnificent Seven: Olive Suspender Buzzer, size 12.

Fig. 212. Once well established, small stillwaters tend to develop increasing buzzer populations provided the trout are not stocked at too high a density.

Bloodwormy Buzzer (Steve Parton)

Fig. 213. Bloodwormy Buzzers, tied by Steve Parton.

During the transition between larval and pupal stages, the features of the developing midge gradually become apparent. Steve Parton uses 'Mill Hill' Japanese Rocaille Seed Beads, the colour being chosen to match the pupae on which the trout are feeding. (So first catch a trout . . . or take a guess!)

A size 8 sproat hook is debarbed and threaded with six or seven beads. A thread stop is then whipped on at the tail and dabbed with Superglue before the beads are slid back one at a time and Superglued together. Next, pale cock pheasant centre-tail fibres are tied in at the eye with sufficient tips protruding forward to bend back as legs. Now tie down the fibres back to the beads and lock the thread in behind the last bead. Dub in claret or red seal's fur for the thorax, tie down, and fit a false hackle of pheasant-tail fibres. To complete Steve's Bloodwormy Buzzer, whip finish the head and the tailstop.

Steve Parton says that for him, 'There is no satisfaction in catching a trout on a Hare's Ear in the middle of a general hatch, because it may have been taken as a representation of a trout pellet. To be worth a damn, your imitation has to work when retrieved at a natural speed in the middle of a preoccupied feed. It has to look like the natural and it has to work repeatedly. You probably haven't got a [worthwhile new] dressing until it has succeeded at least 100 times.'

This fly has proven itself on many more than 100 occasions.

Large summer midges

(*Chironomus plumosus*)

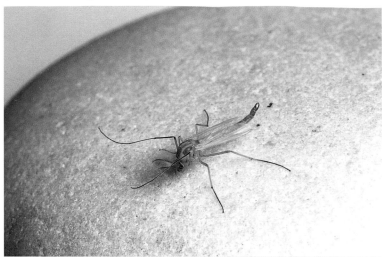

Fig. 214. Large green midge (m).

This species name covers a multitude of flies with distinctly different colouring. The body lengths of the females vary from around 9 mm to 15 mm, while the males, easily distinguished by their feathery (plumosus, or plume-like) antennae, are typically 1 mm shorter.

Males often swarm well away from the water's edge and in such numbers that they can be heard from quite a distance – hence the colloquial name 'buzzers'. Some summer midges emerge in the morning and lay their eggs after sunset. Adult midges live for a few days, and so the occurrence of a good hatch in the morning may not necessarily be a portent of a rise to spent adults that evening: if the weather is unsuitable the females can wait a day or so before mating.

Fig. 215. Large olive midge (f).

Fig. 216. Black midge (m).

Some of the largest midges hatch from very deep water and their larvae, pupae and adults are very dark in colour. When the adults first hatch, however, their wings usually have a distinct ginger tinge.

Magnificent Seven: Greenwell's Glory, size 12 or 14.

Fig. 217. Black midge (f).

Summer midges

Fig. 218. Ginger midge (m).

The chironomid midges illustrated here are from Lough Corrib, where on calm summer evenings wild brown trout up to 5 lb in weight can be caught on imitations of the adult midge. Often, the largest midges hatch during the daytime rather than at dusk, and generally the deeper water is more productive than the shallows.

The larger buzzers tend to trickle off rather than all appear at once, and so rarely is there a general rise of trout to these meaty morsels. When they first hatch there is a gingery appearance to the wings, but this soon disappears. A team of buzzer pupae fished just below the surface sometimes works better than a dry fly in a flat calm, but if there is a good wave a dry fly retrieved slowly can be deadly.

Magnificent seven: Greenwell's Glory, size 12.

Fig. 219. Small green midge (f).

Campto Midge (Peter O'Reilly)

Fig. 220. The Campto Midge, tied by Peter O'Reilly.

There are many colour variations in the summer midges, even within the species *Chironomus plumosus.* Peter O'Reilly has devised a dressing which gives a good match for a particular largish midge which hatches in good numbers on some of the limestone loughs of central Ireland. Midges of similar colour occur elsewhere in the British Isles.

For this pattern, the hook is a size 10 or 12 Kamosan B170, and the tying thread should be primrose or golden olive. The body is dubbed using hare's body fur and then ribbed with fine silver wire. A ginger cree hackle is added next, followed by a head of green DFM (daylight fluorescent material).

Fishing tip
The adult midge spends no time at all on the water once it has emerged from its pupal shuck, but the egg-laying adult *is* worthy of imitation. Midges lay their eggs near the margins, usually after sunset, through the night or early in the morning. The resulting rise is sometimes quite spectacular, but the fish may be very difficult to catch simply because the chances of them taking the artificial fly rather than a natural one are small. Tying an imitation just a little larger than life would seem to improve the odds.

Reed smuts

(*Simulium* species)

These tiny black flies, of which there are many species, are generally less than 3 mm long. This makes it very difficult to imitate them effectively, and because they hatch in enormous numbers they have been dubbed the 'black curse'.

Fig. 221. Reed smuts resting on branched burr reed in the margins of a spate river.

Although some specific imitations do exist, the chances of a fish taking *your* fly rather than one of the many dozens which may also be drifting by each minute are remote. Usually the best tactic when trout are locked onto reed smuts is to offer them either a large black fly – a Hawthorn Fly, for example – or a pattern which contrasts with the hatch. An upwinged dun or a medium-sized sedge fly will sometimes tempt a smutting trout.

Magnificent Seven: no effective imitation.

Fig. 222. These Reed Smuts were tied by Alice Conba on size 26 hooks. During moderate hatches they are useful imitations of the minute 'black curse'.

Grasshoppers and bush crickets

(*Acrididae* and *Tettigoniidae* families)

Fig. 223. A grasshopper from beside an upland stream.

Grasshoppers and crickets are members of the order Orthoptera. Of the 17,000 species in this order, over half are grasshoppers, but only thirty species occur in the British Isles.

The herbivorous grasshopper is plentiful in summer in upland and wooded areas, but pesticides have greatly reduced the numbers in pasture land bordering chalk streams and spate rivers. They vary in colour from palest green through brown to bright red, and the males are often very much smaller than their mates. Effective imitations do exist. The omnivorous bush cricket is equally varied in its mantle but its distribution is more patchy. These insects are mainly nocturnal, and in the British Isles they are largely confined to southern parts.

Magnificent Seven: No effective imitation.

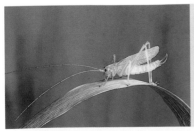

Fig. 224. A bush cricket with its long antennae. This one was found beside a lowland spate river at the tail end of the evening rise.

Soldier beetle

(Cantharis livida)

Fig. 225. The soldier beetle.

Soldier beetles occur in both upland and lowland regions during the summer months. They are usually most abundant in July, when on warm breezy days they get blown onto the surface of rivers and lakes, where they struggle and attract attention to themselves. The closely related sailor beetle, *Cantharis rustica*, is not quite as common. Both seem to prefer unkempt grassland with plenty of wild flowers. Their common names derive from their brightly coloured 'military' uniforms.

These terrestrial beetles have for many years been recognised by flyfishers as worthy of imitation. Skues devised an effective soldier beetle pattern, and Taff Price has devised copies of both species.

Magnificent Seven: Coch-y-bonddu, size 12.

Fig. 226. The sailor beetle in its smart blue 'uniform'.

Soldier Beetle (Taff Price)

Fig. 227. Taff Price's Soldier Beetle.

This soldier beetle imitation, devised by Taff Price, uses orange seal's fur mixed with just a little yellow seal's fur and hare's ear. The hook is a size 14 and the tying thread should be hot orange. The body is ribbed with black tying thread, and the back is orange-brown Raffene. A red cock hackle and a small whip-finished head complete the tying. To represent the darkened area at the rear of the wing case, the Raffene is touched with a black, waterproof pen.

Fishing tip

On hill streams, these kinds of beetle pattern can be very successful on windy summer days. It helps if you cast them in with quite a plop, so as to attract the attention of trout which may not be expecting manna from heaven.

Fig. 228. Trout fishing on a hill stream, where soldier and sailor beetles are plentiful in summer.

Coch-y-bonddu beetle
(*Phyllopertha horticola*)

Fig. 229. Coch-y-bonddu beetles.

Huge numbers of coch-y-bonddu beetles can be seen swarming over the bracken in upland Wales, the north of England and Scotland in mid-summer. Warm, dry weather is needed to bring these beetles out (and a blustery wind to blow them in!). Whenever the weather turns dull and damp, coch-y-bonddu beetles use the bracken fronds as umbrellas, keeping dry until the weather turns more favourable.

Moc Morgan informs me that the true Welsh name of this beetle is coch-a-bon-ddu. Other names include garden chafer, bracken clock and June bug. The thorax varies in colour from mid-green through to black, the latter being the more common in some upland regions.

Magnificent Seven: Coch-y-bonddu, sizes 12 and 14. (What else could we consider using but this traditional Welsh pattern?)

Fig. 230. Good hatches of coch-y-bonddu beetles occur in high summer on the banks of upland lakes and reservoirs.

Large red damsel

(*Pyrrhosoma nymphula*)

Fig. 231. A large red damsel (m).

This is the earliest of the damselflies commonly encountered by still-water flyfishers, and in the south of England a few are usually to be seen before the end of April. From then until the end of summer, adults will be seen flying about the margins whenever the weather is warm and sunny. The females, which are somewhat larger than the males, have a wingspan of nearly 50 mm.

Trout frequently leap in an attempt to interrupt the nuptials of paired damselflies. But it is the nymph, most particularly during its shoreward migration just prior to emerging from the water, which is of greatest importance as far as trout and flyfishers are concerned.

Magnificent Seven, adult: no effective imitation.
nymph: Damsel Nymph.

Fig. 232. The nymph of the large red damselfly.

Common blue damsel

(Enallagma cyathigerum)

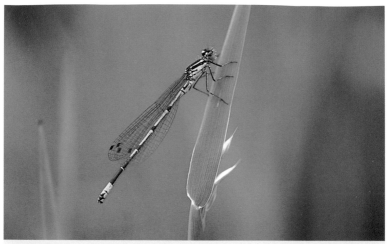

Fig. 233. A common blue damsel (m).

This very common and widespread damselfly is found on most ponds, lakes, canals and slow-flowing rivers in lowland regions. It also occurs on some upland lakes. The wingspan of females of this species is typically 38 mm. The first of these beautiful insects are usually seen in June, and hatches continue each morning throughout the summer and well into autumn.

Several other blue-bodied damsels are found in southern parts of the British Isles; all are members of the *Coenagrion* genus and are relatively rare or localised in their distribution except for the azure damselfly, *Coenagrion puella.*

Magnificent Seven, adult: no effective imitation.
nymph: Damsel Nymph.

Fig. 234. Damsel nymphs are of more interest than damselflies from a fishing viewpoint. This is the nymph of the common blue.

Damsel Nymph (John Wilshaw)

Fig. 235. Damsel Nymph, tied by John Wilshaw.

This damsel nymph is one of John Wilshaw's most successful patterns, and it is particularly effective when lake trout are feeding on damsel nymphs as they migrate towards shallow water just prior to the 'hatch'.

The hook is a size 10, and the other tying details are as follows. The foundation layer is black tying thread, the eyes are lead dumbbells painted either black with a yellow centre or black with a red centre, and the tag is fluorescent green floss, which is also used to rib the body.

A key feature of this fly is its tail, which should be as long as the one illustrated here. This is a plume of marabou, made from approximately equal quantities of light olive marabou and grey marabou fibres. The dubbed body uses the same mixture of marabou fibres. The tying is completed by a partridge hackle, which should be dyed yellow-olive.

Fishing tip
This damsel nymph works particularly well on clear-water fisheries, where takes come 'on the drop' or during a slow but jerky retrieve. John Wilshaw recommends using his Damsel Nymph with either an intermediate or a slow-sink line in order to avoid a trout-scaring wake.

Flying ants

(Formicidae)

Fig. 236. A flying ant.

Ants are social creatures, and some 15,000 species are known. Worker ants remain wingless, but at mating time the sexual forms develop wings and pair in flight. After mating, the females (queens) get rid of their wings and prepare a brood chamber where they spend the rest of their days (and in some cases many years) being fed by the workers and laying eggs.

Flying ant imitations do exist, and a key feature is the egg-timer body shape which is easily replicated with tying thread or silk floss. If you want to experiment, remember that ants have short antennae and no tails.

Just once in a lifetime of flyfishing have I seen a heavy fall of flying ants where the trout fed on them so avidly that the surface of the water boiled. This was on the River Tawe in the Brecon Beacons. Using a Greenwell's Glory I was able to tempt the occasional fish, but I am sure that if I had used a really close imitation, perhaps tied slightly larger than life, I would have enjoyed better sport. The question I must leave unanswered is: should you fill your fly box with patterns to deal with these once-in-a-lifetime opportunities?

Magnificent Seven: Coch-y-bonddu, size 16.

Chapter 6
Autumn and Winter

The transition from summer to autumn can be quite marked: there you are one week fishing flat-calm lakes or rivers which are low and clear and almost lifeless, and the next time you go fishing the lakes and rivers are full . . . of floating leaves, if nothing else! But with the fall, as Americans aptly call this postscript to summer and prelude to winter, there comes a renewal of insect activity. Some of the spring flies (or, in a few cases, species which are very closely related to them) reappear, and other insects begin emerging during the day to cause at least some sort of surface activity.

In this season of mists and mellow fruitfulness, the fishing is generally a little more fruitful than in the dog days of high summer. That is not to say success is in any way guaranteed, because the fishing is now very dependent on weather conditions. On popular fisheries, any trout that have survived all season are by now pretty wise to 'chuck-and-chance-it' tactics, and a more considered approach is usually necessary if you want to catch these clever old stagers.

Fig. 237. A gentle drift in early autumn.

The flies of autumn and winter

One or two summer upwinged flies persist into autumn – the blue-winged olive and the pale watery, for example – but few new ones emerge and none provides such dense hatches as we saw in spring. Stoneflies are increasingly important as the trout season draws to a close, and a dry imitation can provide some excellent fishing, on spate rivers in particular. There are also some really useful autumn sedge flies. Mostly they hatch towards the end of the day when other insect activity is reduced, and if the air does not cool too rapidly these meaty sedges can extend the sport into the evening.

But most of all this is the season of terrestrials. Beetles, daddy-long-legs and a host of other wind-borne creatures drop in on river and lake. And while the fish tend to become more opportunist in autumn, matching the hatch can still be worthwhile, particularly when your aim is to catch those extra-cautious trout whose 'education' through the year has been at your expense!

Then comes the winter, when only occasionally are trout to be seen at all. Most days the stillwater fisheries appear leaden and lifeless. And yet life goes on below the surface as rainbow trout bred to be incapable of breeding continue feeding near the bed of the lake.

For those river fishers lucky enough to have access to a grayling stream, fishing can continue into the new year, with crisp winter mornings offering dry-fly fishing and dull days presenting the ultimate challenge of fishing a deeply sunk nymph.

Fig. 238. Grayling fishing in the Vale of Llangollen.

Autumn dun

(Ecdyonurus dispar)

Fig. 239. Autumn dun (f).

The nymph of the autumn dun is a stone clinger, and like most of the ecdyonurids it sometimes crawls out of the water, usually onto partly submerged stones in the shallows, when the dun is ready to emerge. But autumn duns are also seen hatching at the surface well away from the shallows. In either case, being mixed-weather flies, their entrance into the aerial world can be a boisterous affair, and many autumn duns are sent skittering across the water where they meet a trouty reception committee.

At one time this fly was known as the August dun, and generally it is August before the first significant hatches appear; however, autumn duns are often plentiful through most of September, too.

Although the occasional autumn dun may be seen on the chalk streams, they are most plentiful on stony spate rivers, and when a large hatch occurs the trout can become very determined indeed to chase and capture the skating duns. Some of Ireland's limestone rivers have reasonable hatches of this fly, and they occur also on some large lakes with wind-swept stony shores. Autumn duns are occasionally seen before noon, but the majority of them hatch in the afternoon and early evening.

A dry March Brown provides a close imitation.

Magnificent Seven: Greenwell's Glory, size 14.

Autumn spinner

Fig. 240. Autumn spinner (f).

Male autumn spinners swarm above the margins of the river and are liable to be blown onto the water on blustery days. The females lay their eggs by resting upon stones in the shallows and pushing their abdomens below the surface, attaching the eggs to the sides of the stones below the water level. Spent females inevitably end up floating upon the surface, and when trout rise to them on autumn evenings they usually ignore any smaller flies such as iron blues and purple spinners which may be available at the same time.

The male and female spinners are very similar and do not require separate imitations. A size 14 Pheasant Tail Spinner (page 83) is a reasonably good imitation of the autumn spinner.

Magnificent Seven: Greenwell's Glory, size 14.

Fig. 241. Autumn spinner (m).

Brown sedge

(Anabolia nervosa)

Fig. 242. A brown sedge, *Anabolia nervosa*.

Although the brown sedge first makes an appearance in early summer, the autumn hatches are usually the more prolific. In September great swarms of them are seen over the water, and, with so many flies swirling around, it is inevitable that the occasional traffic accident occurs and flies end up on the water.

This is an important fly both on rivers and on lakes. The larva builds a conical case from sand grains, and to the sides of the case it fixes sticks often much longer than the case itself. This makes the cased larva more difficult for a trout to swallow. (Autopsies show that trout often do swallow these kinds of sedge larvae, and on occasion the sticks can pierce the internal organs of the fish.)

Magnificent Seven: Silver Sedge, size 12 or 14.

Fig. 243. A pair of mating brown sedges (*Hydropsyche* species).

Brown Sedge (Alice Conba)

Fig. 244. Brown Sedge, tied by Alice Conba.

This pattern, devised by Alice Conba of Cahir, makes extensive use of golden pheasant-tail feathers, which provide a very useful mottling effect. The hook is size 12 or size 14, and black tying thread is used.

The ribbing is gold wire, the body hackle is a red-brown cock hackle, and the body itself is eight married herls from a golden pheasant-tail feather. The wings are also golden pheasant-tail, and eight herls are about right here, too. The head hackle is another red cock hackle.

This fly works extremely well as an imitation of brown-bodied sedges with brown or mottled wings – and there are many, including the black and the brown silverhorns and the black sedge, the female of which has dark brown wings.

Fig. 245. A black sedge. (The female often has dark brown wings.)

Caperer

(Helesus radiatus, H. digitatus)

Fig. 246. A caperer, *H. radiatus*.

This is one of the largest sedge flies found in the British Isles, and it is very common both on chalk streams and on spate rivers, where it can provide excellent sport on warm autumn evenings. Both species also occur in stillwaters.

The larva makes its case from pieces of vegetation, often with large sticks cemented along the side. When it is ready, the pupa swims to the surface, where the adult caperer emerges. Adults are to be seen on the wing from mid-August until the end of October.

Specific imitations of the caperer do exist, but I have found none more capable of fooling large brown trout on autumn evenings than the G&H Sedge (page 155) tied with an orange body.

Magnificent Seven: Silver Sedge, size 12.

Fig. 247. Bernard Venables fishing the upper Avon, where the arrival of the caperer is eagerly awaited by trout and trout fishers.

Sandfly

(Rhyacophila dorsalis)

Fig. 248. A sandfly sedge.

This is one of those sedge flies of river and stream which, while some-times seen in small numbers in spring and summer, takes on increasing importance during the autumn months. Its larva is of the free-living type, and, although it spends most of the day tucked away beneath the stones, it is able to swim and does so as it forages for food as dusk descends.

The adults are seen flying mainly in the evenings and they do not tend to swarm; however, on some spate rivers they are sufficiently abundant to justify a reasonably close imitation. A Silver Sedge (page 50) is usually more acceptable than a bulky deer-hair pattern when trout are taking this highly visible fly.

Magnificent Seven: Silver Sedge, size 14.

Fig. 249. The larva of the sandfly sedge, *Rhyacophila dorsalis*, is capable of swimming, albeit with a somewhat inelegant, lashing motion similar to that of a bloodworm.

Needle fly and willow fly

(Leuctra fusca and *Leuctra geniculata)*

Fig. 250. Needle fly.

While the large stoneflies of springtime are the most remarkable in terms of size, appearance and behaviour, the little stoneflies of autumn are of far greater value to flyfishers. The tiny needle fly is mainly found on stony rivers and streams throughout the British Isles, but it is rather less commonly encountered on lakes than is its slightly larger but otherwise very similar cousin the willow fly. The main hatches occur from mid-July until mid-September, and needle flies can be seen laying their eggs from late morning onwards.

The willow fly is particular abundant on the spate rivers of the West Country, Wales, the north of England and parts of Scotland. This fly, unlike most other members of the Plecoptera order, is also fairly common on fast-flowing chalk streams and in the margins of large stony lakes.

Fig. 251. The upper reaches of the River Severn, where autumn stoneflies such as the needle fly occur in vast numbers during the grayling fishing season.

The willow fly

Like other stonefly nymphs, the nymph of the willow fly crawls out of the water when the adult fly is ready to emerge. Egg-laying willow flies and stoneflies are quite definitely worthy of imitation, however, and a size 14 or 16 Snipe and Purple is ideal.

Several other quite similar species hatch in spring, but rarely in such abundance as the autumn stoneflies.

Magnificent Seven: Greenwell's Glory, size 16.

Fig. 252. A 'nymphing' trout.

Fishing tip

When you see a trout holding station on the river bed with its pectoral fins stationary, almost invariably it is a resting fish. If, on the other hand, the pectorals are twitching and the trout is 'on the fin', looking out for drifting nymphs including those of the stoneflies, a suitable nymph or wet fly will often score where a dry fly would not.

Fig. 253. Boulder-strewn spate rivers provide ideal habitat for autumn stoneflies such as the willow fly.

Large crane fly

(Tipula maxima)

Fig. 254. A large crane fly, or daddy-long-legs (m).

The crane flies of spring are mainly the smaller species, many being of aquatic origin, whereas the summer and autumn crane flies include some very big species, most notably *Tipula maxima*, the largest of the crane flies found in the British Isles. These are terrestrial insects, and on warm breezy days great numbers of them are blown onto the water. Lake trout in particular feed avidly and sometimes very selectively on these meaty mouthfuls, and at such times to be without a reasonably good imitation can result in an empty bag.

The males have blunt-ended abdomens and the females have a pointed ovipositor. (Copy the female: use a sharp hook!)

Magnificent Seven: No effective imitation.

Fig. 255. Larvae of many of the small and medium sized crane flies are aquatic, as is this river dweller which is 20 mm long.

Dyffryn Daddy (Derek Hoskin)

Fig. 256. Dyffryn Daddy, tied by Derek Hoskin.

The large size of the daddy-long-legs means that it is possible to include several realistic features in artificial patterns designed to match the hatch. For example, knotted pheasant-tail fibres produce legs which look very similar to the real thing. But one thing spoils most artificial daddy-long-legs patterns, and that is the need for a hackle to help keep the fly afloat.

This imitation, devised by Derek Hoskin, has a detached deer-hair body, legs made from pheasant-tail fibres, and a thorax of etha-foam coloured brown using a waterproof Pantone pen. The wings are cree hackle tips. The Dyffryn Daddy meets the key design requirements of a dry fly: it floats well, it is durable, and trout accept it as the real thing.

Fishing tip
On sunny autumn days when trout refuse to rise to the tiny flies which Nature offers them, a large Dyffryn Daddy left stationary upon the surface will sometimes entice a trout when smaller flies fail. It is usually best to minimise the amount of casting to cover different parts of the surface, since lake trout cruise around slowly even on the brightest of days. It is, of course, important to degrease the leader in such flat calm conditions.

Chapter 7
All the Year Round

Most of the surface food available to trout is seasonal. The transitions between the four seasons are gradual, and surface life alters gradually, too, with many species overlapping spring and summer, summer and autumn, and so on. There are, however, several food creatures which are available in reasonable quantities throughout the year, and they tend to spend most if not all of their time below the surface. In the final chapter in this Part, we will look at a few of the all-the-year-round menu items and their imitation; here it is very much a matter of 'match the munch', because few of these are insects which emerge from the water.

As well as which fly to use, we also need to know where to use it, and, when there is nothing hatching to give us a clue, a certain amount of detective work is needed. Sub-surface food in particular is difficult to locate: it does not necessarily follow the same line as the surface food lanes on a river or the wind lanes on a reservoir. And it may even decide to set up home in different places at different times of the year.

Fig. 257. 'Fishing the water' on a day when no fish are rising.

Changes through the year

Although there is at least some food available to trout at all times, it is important to remember that the appetite of a fish varies considerably with changes in water temperature. In spring and autumn a trout will generally feed more avidly than in summer, when the water temperature may be above the optimum for a comfortable existence (from the trout's point of view). Within the range 10°C to 17°C most trout feed well. When the temperature rises to 18°C or more, brown trout lose their appetites. Rainbow trout will generally tolerate a degree or two more, but then they too become distressed and do not feed at all.

Low temperatures have a similar effect: trout feed very little once the temperature falls below 6°C. Although they can survive for quite long periods at temperatures only just above freezing, in these conditions they become torpid and rest on the bottom, rarely moving at all.

The conclusions from all this are:

- In very cold weather, it is best to move to a part of the fishery where the water temperature is likely to be above average. On sunny days, the shallows will warm up more rapidly than the deeper water; on cold, dull days the only feeding trout may be those near the bed of the very deepest areas, where the water temperature is less prone to fluctuations.

- In hot, sunny weather the shallows will soon become starved of oxygen, and trout will avoid them. During a heat wave, the bed of the deepest water, where the water remains reasonably cool, will be a much better place for daytime fishing. At night, on the other hand, the shallower water cools more rapidly, and some surprisingly large trout can be caught in the shallow margins late at night or just as dawn is breaking.

When fishing during these difficult periods when no trout are rising, it is important to choose the right place at the right time. It is equally important to choose a fly appropriate to the location and depth being fished.

All this may sound pretty obvious, but a great many anglers must spend a great many fruitless hours casting shallow-water food-creature imitations out into deep water, and vice versa. It is an easy mistake to make – I know this because I have done so myself on too many occasions.

Lesser waterboatman

(Corixa species*)*

Fig. 258. A pond-dwelling *Corixa*.

There are more than thirty species of *Corixae* in the British Isles, all very similar in appearance, with boldly patterned backs varying from fawn to dark brown. They live on the beds of lakes and slow-flowing rivers and feed on algae and various organic materials among the silt and debris.

The more important species grow up to a centimetre in length. They use their powerful paddles to swim up to the surface in order to replenish their oxygen supply, stored in the form of a bubble of air adhering to the underside of the body. Depending upon water temperature, journeys to the surface can be as frequent as once in every ten minutes. As a *Corixa* swims to the surface and back, it is most vulnerable to attack by trout or other predators. The main defences of this communal water bug seem to be sheer numbers plus their preference for very shallow water, where the trout themselves may be wary of venturing. Nevertheless, plenty do get taken by trout.

Corixae most frequently appear in trout autopsies in autumn and winter; this may be because the trout are feeding on fry in the shallows and accept them as a welcome 'sweet course'.

Magnificent Seven: GRHE, size 12 or 14.

Corixa (Derek Hoskin)

Fig. 259. Corixa, tied by Derek Hoskin.

When trout are foraging in the muddy margins for these bottom-foraging water bugs there seems little to choose between one *Corixa* pattern and another. Not so, however, in clear-water lakes such as the limestone-rich waters of Langford Fishery beside the River Wylie. There, a closer imitation is necessary. Derek Hoskin developed his Corixa for those difficult situations where a general representation is not good enough.

The hook is size 12, and the tying thread is black. Start with a firm foundation layer of thread before fitting a tag of silver tinsel at the hook bend. Next, flat lead wire or strips cut from the metal foil from a wine bottle are layered on each side of the hook. The woven body is made from brown and white polypropylene yarn, and the legs are provided by six golden pheasant tippet fibres, three on each side of the body. It takes time to tie this fly, but it really does work well.

Fishing tip

Corixae swim up to the surface and down again with jerky movements of their paddle-like front legs. After casting into shallow water and allowing your Corixa to sink to the bottom, retrieve it in a series of short jerks until it reaches the surface then let it sink back down and repeat the process.

Freshwater shrimp

(Gammarus pulex, G. lacustris)

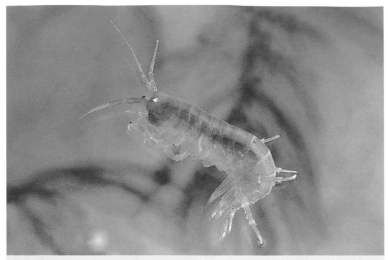

Fig. 260. A freshwater shrimp.

Freshwater shrimps are not, in fact, close relatives of the shrimps of the seashore; they are amphipods, as are sand hoppers. Shrimps occur in a wide variety of waters, from chalk streams and limestone lakes to spate rivers and hill streams, but these crustaceans do need well-oxygenated water and they are most abundant where there is plenty of submerged vegetation. Watercress beds offer the ideal habitat for these communal creatures.

Gammarus pulex is the most commonly encountered species in the British Isles, but there are others including *Crangonyx pseudogracilis*, an introduction from America. This alien freshwater shrimp is a bluey-grey and is less bristly than our native species; it also has the distinction of swimming upright, while *Gammarus* swims on its side.

Freshwater shrimps do not have a particular breeding season, and so adults are available at all times of the year. During mating, the larger males swim with the females tucked under their bodies.

On rivers, shrimps can make up the majority of a trout's food intake during the winter months. Early in the season and towards the end are usually the best times for using a matching artificial.

Magnificent Seven: GRHE, size 12 or 14.

Shrimp (Derek Hoskin)

Fig. 261. Polythene-backed Shrimp, tied by Derek Hoskin.

Derek's Shrimp is heavily weighted using metal foil from the tops of wine bottles, and the shell back is made of polythene cut into a 6-mm wide strip and then stretched until it shrinks to half its original width.

The metal foil is cut into a 2-mm wide strip which is folded and tied down on the top of the hook shank. At this stage a doubled strip of polythene and a length of oval gold tinsel are tied in with maroon thread at the bend of the hook. The dubbed body is a blend of 75 per cent olive green and 25 per cent orange seal's fur (or substitute). Six olive cock hackle fibres are used for the shrimp's feelers, which are tied in to face forward over the eye of the hook.

Next, as the polythene is pulled forward towards the head, the dubbing fibres need to be stroked backwards and downwards. The polythene is then pulled tight and locked down at the head, and a five-turn rib of gold tinsel is wound over it. The second layer of polythene should now be pulled across the back of the shrimp and tied down at the head, where a neat whip finish and two coats of head varnish complete Derek's Shrimp.

Fishing tip
Silty glides with submerged weed beds are the haunts of freshwater shrimps; fish Derek's Shrimp there as you would a nymph.

Water slater

(Asellus aquaticus, A. meridianus)

Fig. 262. A water slater, or water hog louse.

The water slater, sometimes called the water hog louse, is a close relative of the woodlouse. This crustacean is generally found where there are large amounts of rotting wood and leaves. It is able to survive in water with a much lower oxygen level than the freshwater shrimp could tolerate. Small ponds and tree-lined lakes are the most likely places to find water slaters, but they do also occur in some slow-flowing rivers and streams.

Despite the fact that water slaters sometimes occur in quite large numbers, they are not often a significant contributor to the food supply of trout. It is unlikely, therefore, that you will need a close imitation of the water slater, and to date this creature has received little attention from fly tyers.

The very nature of the habitat of water slaters makes it difficult to present a matching artificial fly without getting snagged on the bottom or the fly collecting dead leaves or other debris which would spoil its effectiveness as an imitation. In the event that you should need to imitate this creature, a reasonably good general representation can be achieved with a Gold-ribbed Hare's Ear.

Magnificent Seven: GRHE, size 14.

Water snails

Fig. 263. The wandering snail, *Limnaea peregna*.

Lake trout are not averse to eating water snails complete with their shells and, as these molluscs can occur in great abundance in shallow, weedy stillwaters, artificial snails can be an effective means of catching trout. The greatest concentrations of snails generally occur in limestone-rich waters, but many species are able to live in neutral and mildly acidic waters. The wandering snail, *Limnaea peregna*, is one such example; it feeds on detritus on the beds of shallow pools and slow-flowing rivers.

The river snail, *Viviparus viviparus*, is found mainly in rivers in the south of England, while the great ramshorn snail, *Planorbis corneus*, is mainly confined to hard-water lakes. Imitations made of cork or Raffene can be effective when allowed to drift in the margins.

Magnificent Seven: No effective imitation.

Fig. 264. A ramshorn snail.

Crayfish

(Austropotamobius pallipes)

Fig. 265. A crayfish.

The crayfish, a relative of the marine lobster, is a decapod – it has ten legs. The two front ones are larger than the others and carry a pair of powerful claws, used for catching and cutting up food. For the most part, crayfish are scavengers, but they do occasionally seize and kill small fishes and even other crayfish.

In the limestone-rich waters where crayfish are plentiful, the trout grow large. Once a fish gets to over 1 lb in weight, it tends to rise less frequently for surface food and to take more of its meals in bed. On the river bed or on the bed of a limestone lake, crayfish lurk beneath ledges and among weed beds, and that is where the big trout feed.

Crayfish are at their most vulnerable immediately after they moult, because then they are soft and defenceless. In their first three or four years, young crayfish moult many times; thereafter they moult annually, in autumn.

Artificial crayfish 'flies' are difficult to cast, but they certainly work well. They are fished to swim backwards, which is quite appropriate because a threatened crayfish does just that, with its claws raised in a defensive posture.

Magnificent Seven: No effective imitation.

Crayfish (Peter Masters)

Fig. 266. Crayfish, tied by Peter Masters.

Time was when you could visit any chalk stream and see our native white-footed crayfish; today they are more localised, and in some areas they have been ousted by an alien species, the more aggressive American signal crayfish. Peter Masters ties a pretty good general representation of a recently moulted, immature crayfish of either species – the equivalent of peeler crabs to the sea angler.

The hook is a size 8 long shank, and the tying thread is black. The other materials, in the sequence in which they are tied in, are as follows:

Feelers: two pheasant-tail fibres.
Eyes: 50-lb b.s. black nylon burnt at each end to form a dumb-bell.
Claws: grouse body feathers, varnished and clipped to form a V.
Body: a mixture of natural and olive hare's ear wound after spinning on a dubbing loop of thin copper wire.
Legs: A grouse body feather set along the back and trapped in place by the back cover.
Back cover: strip of light blue plastic bag or a strip of organza
Rib: black tying thread.

Once the back material has been pulled tight to the eye, it is tied down with a whip finish. This, plus the ribbing, secures the legs.

Three-spined stickleback

(Gasterosteus aculeatus)

Fig. 267. A three-spined stickleback in its summer colours.

The three-spined stickleback is found in all kinds of waters, including rivers, canals, lakes and estuaries, but always in the slow or stillwater areas. A related species, the tiny nine-spined stickleback *(Pungitius pungitius)*, is the smallest of the freshwater fishes found in the British Isles. (In reality a fish of this species can have anything between seven and twelve spines.) Less common than the three-spined stickleback, it is mainly confined to weedy stillwaters and estuaries.

Sticklebacks spawn in the spring, when the males develop a bright red belly and their eyes turn blue. These little creatures are unique in that the males build nests, rather like birds' nests, out of vegetation; then they perform courtship dances to entice females into their nests. Once the eggs have hatched, the adult sticklebacks care for their young during the first few weeks of life.

The life-span of a stickleback is typically three to four years, but they are at their most vulnerable at the fry stage, when their immature armour provides little or no protection. Marauding trout will dash into a shoal of sticklebacks, stunning several of them before tucking into a leisurely meal.

Magnificent Seven: Damsel Nymph.

Polystickle (Richard Walker)

Fig. 268. The Polystickle.

Purists who view with disdain the lure fisher might pause to consider who is most closely matching the munch. Arguably, some of the modern fish imitations come a lot closer to Nature's creations than any upwinged dun or spinner that ever came from a fly dresser's vice. Certainly, there are days when, if it scanned the surface from dawn through to dusk, a trout might never see a floating insect; but the small fish are always there. Hungry trout are not purists!

Richard Walker was not one to let prejudice cloud his creative thinking, and he has left us with several successful fly patterns. When Walker devised this particular fly, in the 1960s, he called it the Sticklefly. Ken Sinfoil further developed the concept, incorporating a polythene body – hence the name Polystickle.

The hook is a long-shank size 6 or 8, and the tying thread is black. Crimson floss silk is used for the front quarter of the body and clear polythene strip makes up the remainder. The back and tail are of brown Raffene, and a hot orange beard hackle and varnished head complete the fly. Eyes can be added to the head if you wish.

Fishing tip
When a Polystickle is fished just under the surface with a jerky retrieve, it looks and behaves very much like an injured stickleback in spawning colours.

Minnow

(Phoxinus phoxinus)

Fig. 269. A shoal of minnows in their autumn colours.

Minnows are the smallest members of the carp family found in the British Isles, and rarely grow to more than 10 cm in length. Provided the water is clean and reasonably well oxygenated, minnows can live in a wide variety of habitats, including chalk streams and spate rivers, but are not often found in small stillwaters. They are shoal fish and are preyed upon by kingfishers, otters, and other fish eaters including trout.

Artificial minnows have long been used as spinning baits, but there are also several successful fly patterns, including the Muddler Minnow with its spun deer-hair head and brown 'wing'.

Magnificent Seven: Damsel Nymph.

Fig. 270. These fish fry imitations make use of rabbit fur to suggest moving fins and woven mylar to represent body scales.

Deer-hair Fry (Peter Gathercole)

Fig. 271. Deer-hair Fry, tied by Peter Gathercole.

Angling author and photographer Peter Gathercole has secured a world-wide reputation for the quality and creativity of his fly tying. Peter has also made a special study of waterlife, and his imitations of the creatures on which trout feed are among the most realistic. Generally, his patterns are not difficult to tie; however, a lot of work goes in to the dressing of one of Peter's Deer-hair Fry.

The fly illustrated here is an imitation roach fry. It was produced by spinning deer hair onto a long-shank hook and then clipping it to the required outline. (With care and patience it is even possible to replicate the fins.) The realistic colours are applied using Pantone permanent marker pens. Marabou is used for the tail.

Fishing tip

Trout are, by nature, lazy creatures, and so when it comes to attacking shoals of fry they invariably single out any weak or injured specimens rather than chasing after the fitter and more agile ones. And because sick fish so frequently end up struggling on the surface, this is usually the best place to offer your artificial fly. An intermediate line enables you to offer your lure at the surface while avoiding the disturbance of line wake which would occur if you were to use a floater. Alternatively, use a floating line and simply allow the roach fry to drift on the breeze just like a dead fish.

A fly for all seasons

Pheasant Tail Nymph (Frank Sawyer)

Fig. 272. A Pheasant Tail Nymph, tied by Mrs Frank Sawyer.

At the beginning of this book I posed several questions which have troubled flyfishers through the ages. One of these is: is there a sensible way of choosing an artificial fly when nothing at all is hatching or falling onto the water? Since this can be the case in spring, summer, autumn or winter, we could say that we need a 'fly for all seasons'.

The most obvious conclusion when there is no hatch or fall of flies is that trout will not be able to feed at the surface at such times, and so they must settle for what they can find beneath the surface. Most of the sub-surface food lives very close to the bottom, and so a fly for all seasons should be a weighted pattern.

We also know that many of the nymphs and larvae live under stones, deep inside weed beds or hidden away in tunnels in the sand and silt. The exceptions are the torpedo-shaped nymphs – the *Baëtis* olives, the lake olive and the large summer dun are examples. The Pheasant Tail Nymph is an excellent representation of the darker members of this group of agile darters which are available to trout at all times.

Frank Sawyer's PTN was tied with pheasant-tail fibres and copper wire. It remains one of the most popular and widely used nymphs, and is simplicity itself to tie – the best flies so often are.

A fly for all reasons

Palmer Nymph (Conrad Voss Bark)

Fig. 273. Palmer Nymph, tied by Conrad Voss Bark.

Many theories have been put forward as to why trout – stillwater trout in particular – find this fly attractive. Conrad himself suspects that it worked well at Two Lakes and at Blagdon because the trout had been feeding upon freshwater shrimps; Richard Walker, an inveterate leg puller, said that Palmer Nymphs looked more like water lice; and I remarked to the originator that his fly bore more than a passing resemblance to an ascending sedge pupa. The last word must remain with the inventor: 'It is an impressionist fly.'

But not really the last word: that belongs to the trout, whose judgement when there is no obvious single source of food to lock onto is that the Palmer Nymph will do nicely.

The hook is usually a size 12, and the tying thread should be brown. On a varnished foundation layer, tie in fine wire at the tail to hold down the palmered body hackle. Tie in fine lead wire at the centre of the hook shank and wind it to just behind the head. Next tie in greeny-yellow floss at the tail and bring it towards the head to make a well-shaped body. Now tie in yellow ostrich herl at the head and hackle it down to the tail. The fine wire holds down this herl and is then wound through to the head and tied off. Tie in an olive green hackle at the head and take five turns in front of the ostrich herl. A neat whip finish completes the Palmer Nymph.

Part III
The DIY Entomologist

Chapter 8
Further Investigations

If you want to learn more about the creatures on which trout feed, the easiest way is to study them at close quarters. One of the best investments is an aquarium – better still, why not have several?

Making an aquarium

Many products come packed in clear plastic containers, which make ideal aquariums. Alternatively you can make a glass aquarium, using clear silicone sealant to hold the pieces together. Small aquariums are best: insects have too much room to hide in large ones. In a confined space it is easier to keep a close eye on the contents.

To keep nymphs and larvae for more than a few hours, it is vital to maintain a good supply of oxygen. A small electric aerator with a system of valves and plastic pipes will feed several aquariums, so the setting-up cost per aquarium can be very little. The running cost of such a low-power device is also quite minimal.

With an aerator running, even fast-water nymphs such as the march brown can be kept for several weeks so that you can observe them emerging as duns and finally metamorphosing into spinners.

Fig. 274. This chocolate box has become a useful aquarium.

Capturing nymphs, larvae and winged insects

Many kinds of aquatic larvae and nymphs can be collected by drawing an aquarium net through weed beds. Alternatively, a piece of net curtain stapled between a pair of broom handles will collect nymphs as they drift downstream naturally (or in much greater quantities with a little help from a friend disturbing the weeds upstream of the net).

When collecting 'kick samples' from under stones on fast-flowing rivers, something rather more robust may be needed. A flour sieve taped firmly to a broom handle is just the job. Have a large enough water container so that you can immerse the sieve fully to shake out your catch, or you may find that counting the (remaining) tails is no guide to identifying the species!

For capturing winged insects, you could try a large aquarium net swept through the bankside grasses; however, more often than not the flies you want will be above head height, and they are amazingly adept at swerving away from danger. A large butterfly net, of the type supplied by specialist firms such as Watkins and Doncaster, increases considerably the prospects of success.

Swarming sedge flies are easy to catch, but the larger, solitary sedges which emerge at dusk are more difficult unless you can find their daytime roosts. An altogether more effective method is to use a trap. This is simply an ultra-violet lamp in a box with a perspex lid. The sedge flies are attracted to the light and enter the box via a hole in the lid. You will, of course, also collect moths, midges and many other kinds of insects.

Fig. 275. 'Would you like to see my lamp collection?'

Close observation

Once your aquariums are operational, you will have plenty of opportunity to observe insect behaviour. If you have been selective in stocking, the beetle larvae, dragonfly nymphs and greater water boatmen will be separated from the creatures on which they normally prey; if not, you will soon have just a few very plump specimens.

Nymph to dun

Include some large stones so that those nymphs which leave the water when the adults are ready to emerge have got somewhere to clamber out. Once you see a nymph leaving the water, stick around. In a very short time the outer skin will split and the fly will crawl out, pump blood into its wings and make its maiden flight. It will need somewhere dry to land, of course – a few marginal plants or a bit of driftwood will do – otherwise it may fall back into the water.

Most of the agile darting nymphs and several of the others simply swim up and the dun emerges onto the surface. You can observe this if you are very patient. There is another way, and that is to use a video camera. Leave it running for an hour or so; then check the aquarium to see if any flies have emerged. If so, there will be a few seconds of really interesting activity somewhere in that hour of film; fast forward to find it. If no flies hatched, rewind and run the tape again. When filming live nymphs, use a very thin aquarium so that the nymphs cannot keep moving in and out of focus. I made mine from a pair of miniature picture frames.

Fig. 276. A video camera films duns as they emerge.

Dun to spinner

Most duns rest for a day or more before changing into spinners, and so watching and waiting is hardly worth while. Instead, put a few duns into a box and store them in the refrigerator for two or three days. Bring them out and observe closely: within a minute or two they will warm up, take their overcoats off and . . . magic: the transformation from dun to spinner takes place before your eyes.

Other orders

Upwinged flies are particularly difficult to study because the nymph-to-dun transition often occurs very quickly; however, sedge flies, stoneflies and damselfies become adults more slowly, giving you time to focus your camera and take a sequence of shots.

Following in giants' footsteps

If you have not yet read *The Trout and the Fly* by Brian Clarke and John Goddard, do get a copy. In it you will learn about their experiments (building upon the much earlier findings of E M Harding) to test various theories about the appearance of natural and artificial flies on the surface of the water. If your aquarium has one side sloping at 45 degrees, you will be able to repeat some of these experiments and to see at first hand which of your own fly patterns stand up to close scrutiny from the trout's point of view.

Fig. 277. An aquarium with a sloping side is used to study flies in the mirror and in the window.

Appendix I: Identity Parade

There are some excellent keys available to help in identifying insects, in many instances right down to particular species. In the limited space available here, there is only room for a basic guide to the most commonly encountered flies. In most cases, this is all you will need; however, at the end of the book there is a list of recommended further reading which includes some of the scientific keys.

For now, let's suppose you have found an insect and you want to identify and match it. Here is what you can do:

1. Check the table opposite to find which order the insect belongs to.
2. If the insect is in an aquatic stage of its life-cycle (nymph, larva or pupa) and you want to determine the genus and species, you will need to refer to scientific keys. To determine the exact species you may have to use a microscope.
3. For winged insects, which are of most interest to flyfishers who want to match the hatch, proceed as follows. From knowledge of the season of the year when you saw the fly, turn to the appropriate chapter of the book – Spring, Summer, or Autumn and Winter – where trout food sources are listed in the sequence Ephemeroptera, Tricoptera, Plecoptera, Diptera, insects from various other orders, and then other creatures on which trout feed. Use the illustrations to find the closest match.
4. Check the text for an appropriate matching fly – either one of the Magnificent Seven or perhaps a close imitation from the 'Deadly Dozen' described in Appendix II.

Fig. 278. What kind of fly am I?

Identifying the order of an insect

Nymphs and larvae	Most likely to be
Three short tails; plate or filament gills along sides	Upwing (Ephemeroptera)
Two tails	Stonefly nymph (Plecoptera)
One tail	Alder larva (Neuroptera) or beetle larva (Plecoptera)
Caterpillar-like	Uncased caddis or sedge fly larva (Tricoptera)
Caterpillar-like, encased in sand, pebbles, bits of vegetation, etc	Cased caddis or sedge fly larva (Tricoptera)
Worm-like body with small protrusions at each end	Chironomid midge larva, or bloodworm (Diptera)
Seven-segmented body with large 'head' and what looks like a pair of ears	Chironomid midge pupa (Diptera)
Three broad 'tails'; long body; very large eyes	Damsel nymph (Odonata)

Winged insects	Most likely to be
Two or three long tails; large dull upright wings, possibly with a pair of smaller hindwings	Upwinged dun (Ephemeroptera)
Two or three very long tails; large translucent upright wings, possibly with smaller hindwings	Upwinged spinner (Ephemeroptera)
Two short tails; four shiny wings laid along body	Stonefly (Plecoptera)
Four hairy wings held in ridge-tent shape; no tails	Sedge fly (Tricoptera)
Four shiny wings held in ridge-tent shape; no tails	Alder fly (Neuroptera)
No tails; two wings held in a V or folded flat across body	True fly (Diptera)
Long, thin body; four equal length wings held along body; large eyes	Damselfly (Odonata)

Families, genera and species of the most common of the upwinged flies (Ephemeroptera)

Family	Family characteristics
Ephemeriidae	Burrowing nymphs; adults very large with large upright hindwings and three tails
Heptageniidae	Stone clinger nymphs; adults have large, upright hindwings and two tails
Leptophebiidae	Laboured swimmer nymphs; adults are darkish with large upright hindwings and three tails
Ephemerellidae	Moss creeper nymphs; adults lightish with large upright hindwings and three tails
Baëtidae	Agile darter nymphs; adults are smallish, with small oval hindwings or no hindwings, and two tails
Siphlonuridae	Agile darter nymphs; adults very large and dark with large hindwings and two tails
Caënidae	Silt crawler nymphs; adults mainly white or grey and very small, with three tails and no hindwings

Genus	Species	Common name	Page
Ephemera	*danica; vulgata*	Mayfly	85
Rithrogena	*semicolorata*	Olive upright	70
	germanica	March brown	66
Ecdyonurus	*dispar*	Autumn dun	182
	torrentis	Large brook dun	76
	venosus	Late march brown	66
	insignis	Large green dun	140
Heptagenia	*sulphurea*	Yellow may	73
	lateralis	Dusky yellowstreak	142
Leptophlebia	*vespertina*	Claret dun	78
	marginata	Sepia dun	78
Paraleptophlebia	*cincta*	Purple dun	144
	submarginata	Turkey brown	84
Ephemerella	*ignita*	Blue-winged olive	134
Baëtis	*rhodani*	Large dark olive	58
	atrebatinus	Dark dun	58
	vernus; buceratus	Medium olive	124
	scambus	Small dark olive	126
	fuscatus	Pale watery	114
	muticus; niger	Iron blue	62
Cloëon	*diptera*	Pond olive	132
	simile	Lake olive	128
Procloëon	*bifidum*	Pale evening dun	122
Centroptilum	*luteolum*	Small spurwing	118
Pseudo-centroptilum	*pennulatum*	Large spurwing	120
Siphlonurus	*lacustris*	Large summer dun	148
Caënis	*horaria; robusta; macrura; luctuosa; rivulorum*	Caënis fly	145
Brachycercus	*harrisella*		

Fly selection guide for upwinged duns and spinners

Natural Insect	General Representation	
	Dun	Spinner
Mayfly	Greenwell's Glory	Greenwell's Glory
Olive upright		
March brown		
Autumn dun		
Large brook dun		
Late march brown		
Large green dun		
Yellow may	Tups Indispensable	Tups Indispensable
Dusky yellowstreak	Greenwell's Glory	Greenwell's Glory
Claret dun		
Sepia dun		
Purple dun		
Turkey brown		
Blue-winged olive		Tups Indispensable
Large dark olive		
Dark dun		
Medium olive		
Small dark olive		
Iron blue		Greenwell's Glory
Pond olive		Tups Indispensable
Lake olive		
Pale watery	Tups Indispensable	
Pale evening dun		
Small spurwing		
Large spurwing		
Large summer dun	Greenwell's Glory	Greenwell's Glory
Caënis fly	Tups Indispensable	Tups Indispensable

Close Matching Artificial		Hook
Dun	**Female Spinner**	size
Mayfly Dun (Masters)	No Hook Spinner	10
Olive Upright (Mawle)	Olive Upright (Mawle)	14
March Brown	Ecdyonurid Spinner (Greenhalgh)	12
		12
		12
		12
		12
Sparkle Dun (Weaver)	Sparkle Dun (Weaver)	12
Claret Dun (Harris)	Pheasant Tail Spinner or Polythene-winged Spinner (Clarke)	14
		14
		14
		14
		14
Imperial (Kite) or Duck's Dun (Jardine) or Funneldun (Patterson)	Sherry Spinner (Lunn)	14
	Pheasant Tail Spinner or Polythene-winged Spinner (Clarke)	14
		14
		16
		18
Iron Blue Dun (Russell)	Houghton Ruby (Lunn)	16
Lake Olive (Masters)	Lunn's Particular (Lunn)	16
		16
Duck's Dun (Jardine) or Funneldun (Patterson)	Polythene-winged Spinner (Clarke)	16
		16
		18
		14
		10
Caënis (Conba)	Caënis (Conba)	22

Appendix II: The Deadly Dozen

If you tie your own flies, you can match the hatch the way the experts do. Why not tie up some of the Deadly Dozen patterns described and illustrated in this book?

1 **Duck's Dun or Funneldun (light/medium) or Clonanav CDC**
   for pale watery, spurwing and pale evening duns; and for medium olive, small dark olive, b-w o, pond and lake olive duns.

2 **Duck's Dun or Funneldun (dark)**
   for claret, sepia, purple and turkey brown duns; large dark olive and iron blue; march brown, autumn, large brook, late march brown, large green, dusky yellowstreak and large summer duns.

3 **Sparkle Dun (Mike Weaver)**
   for the dun and spinner of the yellow may.

4 **Mayfly Dun (Peter Masters)**
   for the dun and egg-laying spinner of the mayfly.

5 **Polythene-winged Spinner (Brian Clarke)**
   for all spent spinners.

6 **Conba Caënis**
   for caënis duns and spinners.

7 **Hawthorn (Jon Beer) or Black Gnat (Peter O'Reilly)**
   for hawthorn and heather flies, black gnats, adult midges, most stoneflies and dark beetles.

8 **Deveaux Sedge or Conba Sedge**
   for all sedge flies.

9 **Bloodwormy Buzzer (Steve Parton) or Olive Suspender Buzzer**
   for all buzzer pupae.

10 **Damsel Nymph (John Wilshaw)**
   for all damsel nymphs.

11 **Deer-hair Fry (Peter Gathercole)**
   for all small fishes.

12 **Gold-ribbed Hare's Ear**
   because this traditional nymph pattern has not been surpassed.

With this selection, in a range of sizes, you can count yourself well equipped to match the hatch. Tight lines and singing reels!

Further Reading

Resulting from the research of professional and amateur entomologists and biologists, there is available today an enormous amount of information on aquatic insects and other creatures which trout feed upon. Much of this research has been written up in scientific journals and may be difficult for us ordinary flyfishers to understand; however, some of the finest of entomologists have, perhaps not entirely by chance, also been keen anglers, and they have produced summaries and identification keys which are both readable and informative. As the scope of this book is necessarily limited (as, indeed, is the competence of its author) it may be helpful to list some further reading for those keen to learn more about this subject.

Books on aquatic insects and other waterlife
John Goddard, *Trout Flies of Britain and Europe*, A&C Black, 1991
   John Goddard is Britain's leading authority on aquatic flies and their imitation, and he has written several books on the subject. This beautifully illustrated volume contains the results of research and observations reported in his earlier book plus a valuable introduction to flies encountered only on mainland Europe.

Cyril O Hammond, *The Dragonflies of Britain and Europe*, Harley Books, 1983.
   This book includes distribution maps and keys to common and rare species of dragonflies and damselflies.

J R Harris, *An Angler's Entomology*, Collins, 1952.
   This book is a classic, covering the identification, behaviour and distribution of flies, and some aspects of trout fishing. It is particularly detailed on the upwinged flies.

T T Macan and E B Worthington, *Life in Lakes and Rivers*, Collins, 1951.
   Macan and Worthington, scientists working at the Freshwater Biological Association's laboratory on Lake Windermere, cover the whole gamut of waterlife including water chemistry, plants, algae, insects and other animals, as well as fishes.

Frank Sawyer, *Nymphs and the Trout*, A&C Black, 1958.
   This records a life-long study, mainly on the Hampshire Avon.

Robin Smith, *Life of the Ponds and Streams in Britain, vols I & II*, Jarrold & Sons, 1979.
   These little booklets provide an ideal introduction for young people with an interest in water life.

Dave Whitlock, *A Guide to Aquatic Trout Food*, Swan Hill, 1994
   Although this is an American perspective on the subject, much of the content is relevant to flyfishing in the British Isles.

Freshwater Biological Association booklets

The FBA series of scientific publication is extensive. Listed here are some of particular interest to the amateur angler-entomologist.

J M Elliot and U H Humpesch, *A Key to the Adults of the British Ephemeroptera*.

H B N Hynes, *Nymphs of the British Stoneflies*.

D E Kimmins, *Adults of the Ephemeroptera*.

T T Macan, *British Water Bugs*.

T T Macan, *A Key to the Adults of the British Tricoptera*.

T T Macan, *Nymphs of the Ephemeroptera*.

Imitative flyfishing

Bob Church and Peter Gathercole, *Fly Fishing for Trout*, Crowood, 1995.

Brian Clarke, *The Pursuit of Stillwater Trout*, A&C Black, 1975.

John Goddard and Brian Clarke, *The Trout and the Fly*, Benn, 1980.

Malcolm Greenhalgh, *Trout Fishing in Rivers*, Witherby, 1987.

Charles Jardine, *Dark Pools*, Crowood Press, 1991.

Oliver Kite, *Nymph Fishing in Practice*, Herbert Jenkins, 1963.

Pat O'Reilly, *Tactical Flyfishing*, Crowood Press, 1990.

Taff Price, *Tying and Fishing the Sedge*, Blandford, 1994.

John Roberts, *To Rise a Trout*, Crowood Press, 1988.

Artificial flies

A Courtney Williams, *A Dictionary of Trout Flies*, A&C Black, 1949.

Mike Dawes, *The Flytier's Companion*, Swan Hill, 1992.

Peter O'Reilly, *The Trout and Salmon Flies of Ireland*, Merlin Unwin, 1995.

John Roberts, *The New Illustrated Dictionary of Trout Flies*, Allen & Unwin, 1986.

Keith Robson, *Robson's Guide*, Beekay, 1985.

Reading just for pleasure

There are so many flyfishing books that are a delight to read, but here are just a few I am sure you will enjoy.

Bryan Hammond (Ed), *Halcyon Days*, Swan Hill, 1992.

Neil Patterson, *Chalkstream Chronicle*, Merlin Unwin, 1995.

Harry Plunket-Greene, *Where the Bright Waters Meet*, 1924.

Bernard Venables, *Autobiography of a Fisherman*, Merlin Unwin, 1994.

Conrad Voss Bark, *A History of Flyfishing*, Merlin Unwin, 1992.

Index

General

Bardogs Aldie 109
Bead-head Damsel Nymph 51
Beer, Jon 105
Beetles 36
Bell, Howard 153
Black Gnat, dry fly 107
Bloodworm, imitation 163
Bloodwormy Buzzer 165
Caddis Pupa, imitation 153
Caënis, dry fly 147
Campto Midge 169
Claret Dun, dry fly 81
Clarke, Brian 117, 213
Clonanav CDC Dun 137
Coch-y-bonddu Beetle 52,
Conba, Alice 139, 147, 170
Corixa, imitation 195
Crayfish, imitation 201
Deer-hair Fry 205
Deveaux Sedge 157
Downs, Donald 109
Duck's Dun 123
Duck Fly, emerger 103
Dyffryn Daddy 191
Ecdyonurid Spinner,
   dry fly 141
Flat-winged flies 32
Funneldun 115
G&H Sedge 155
Gathercole, Peter 205
Goddard, John 117, 213
Gold-ribbed Hare's Ear 47
Grannom, dry fly 93
Greenhalgh, Malcolm 141
Greenwell's Glory 48
Grey, Melvin 101
Harding, E M 213
Harris, J R 81, 221
Hawthorn Fly, dry fly 105
Hoskin, Derek 191, 195
Houghton Ruby 65
Iron Blue Dun, dry fly 63
Jackson, Nigel 63
Jardine, Charles 123
Jones, Steffan 51
Kite, Oliver 61
Kite's Imperial 61
Lake Olive, dry fly 129
Large Stonefly, dry fly 101

Lunn, Albert 131
Lunn, William 65, 131
Lunn's Particular 131
Marabou-tailed Tadpole 111
March Brown, dry fly 69
Masters, Peter 89, 129, 201
Mawle, Guy 71
Mayfly Dun, dry fly 89
Mayfly Nymph, artificial 87
No Hook Spinner 91
Nymphs, adaptation 23
O'Reilly, Peter 107, 169
Olive Suspender Buzzer 53
Olive Upright, dry fly 71
Palmer Nymph 207
Parton, Steve 165
Patterson, Neil 115, 222
Pheasant Tail Nymph, 206
Pheasant Tail Spinner 83
Polystickle 203
Polythene-backed Shrimp 197
Polythene-winged Spinner 117
Price, Taff 173
Reed Smut, dry fly 170
Riegen, John 91
Rubbery Caddis 151
Russell, Pat 93
Ryan, Andrew 137, 157
Sawyer, Frank 17, 206
Sedge flies 27
Sherry Spinner, dry fly 139
Silver Sedge 50
Snipe and Purple 97
Stoneflies 30
Terrestrial insects 113, 181
Thorax Hackle Dun 75
Trout, nymphing 189
Trout, senses of 16
Trout vision 10
Tups Indispensable 49
Upwinged flies 22
Venables, Bernard 47, 186
Voss Bark, Conrad 207
Walker, Richard 203, 207
Water bugs 42
Weaver, Mike 75
Wilshaw, John 163, 177
Wotton, Davy 153
Yellow May Sparkle Dun 75

Common Names

Alder fly 108
Ant 178
Autumn dun 182
Backswimmer 42
Banded demoiselle 40
Black gnat 106
Black midge 102, 167
Black sedge 95
Bloodworm 162
Blue-winged olive 134
Broad-bodied chaser 39
Brown sedge 184
Brown silverhorn sedge 156
Bush cricket 171
Caënis fly 145
Caperer 186
Cinnamon sedge 152
Claret dun 78
Coch-y-bonddu beetle 174
Cranefly 32, 190
Crayfish 200
Daddy-long-legs 191
Damsel, common blue 41
Damsel, common red 174
Damsel nymph 175, 176
Dragonfly nymph 38
Dragonfly, red darter 38
Dragonfly, southern hawker 39
Dusky yellowstreak 142
February red 96
Freshwater shrimp 197
Ginger midge 168
Grasshopper 171
Grannom sedge 92
Great diving beetle 36
Great red sedge 154
Greater waterboatman 42
Green midge 168
Grouse wing sedge 159
Hawthorn fly 104
Heather fly 104
Iron blue 62
Jenny spinner 64
Lake olive 128
Large brook dun 76
Large cinnamon sedge 150
Large dark olive 58
Large green dun/spinner 140
Large spurwing 120

Large summer dun 148
Large yellow sally 160
Late march brown 66
Lesser waterboatman 194
Little sky blue 118
Marbled sedge 158
March brown 66
Mayfly 85
Medium olive 124
Minnow 204
Needle fly 188
Olive buzzer pupa 35, 53
Olive upright 70
Pale evening dun 122
Pale watery 114
Phantom midge larva 162
Pond olive 132
Pond skater 42
Purple dun 144
Ramshorn snail 199
Red darter dragonfly 38
Reed smut 170
Sailor beetle 172
Sandfly 187
Sepia dun 78
Sherry spinner 138
Small dark olive 126
Small spurwing 118
Small yellow sally 161
Soldier beetle 172
Southern hawker 39
Stick insect 43
Stickleback 44, 202
Tadpole 110
Turkey brown 84
Wandering snail 199
Water bug 42
Water measurer 42
Water slater 128
Welshman's button 149
Willow fly 188
Yellow may dun 73
Yellow sally 160
Yellow spotted sedge 94
Yellow upright spinner 72

Scientific Names

Acrididae 171
Aeschna cyanea 39
Anabolia nervosa 184
Anthripsodes species 156
Anthripsodes albifrons 156
Aphelocheirus montandoni 43
Asellus aquaticus 198
Asellus meridianus 198
Austropotamobius pallipes 200
Baëtis atrebatinus 60
Baëtis fuscatus 114
Baëtis muticus 62
Baëtis niger 62
Baëtis rhodani 58
Baëtis scambus 126
Baëtis tenax 124
Baëtis vernus 124
Bibio johannis 106
Bibio marci 104
Bibio pomonae 104
Brachycentrus subnubilis 92
Brachycercus harisella 145
Brachyptera risi 96
Bufo bufo 110
Caënis species, 145
Caënis macrura 145
Calopteryx splendens 40
Cantharis livida 35, 172
Cantharis rustica 35
Centroptilum luteolum 118
Centroptilum pennulatum 120
Chaoborus species 162
Chironomid species 102, 162
Chironomus plumosus 167
Chloroperla torrentium 161
Cloëon dipterum 132
Cloëon simile 133
Corixa species 194
Dytiscus marginalis 36
Ecdyonurus dispar 182
Ecdyonurus insignis 140
Ecdyonurus torrentis 76
Ecdyonurus venosus 66
Enalagma cyathigerum 41, 176
Ephemera danica 85
Ephemera vulgata 85
Ephemerella ignita 134

Formicidae 178
Gammarus lacustris 196
Gammarus pulex 196
Gasterosteus aculeatus 202
Gerris species 42
Helesus digitatus 186
Helesus radiatus 186
Heptagenia lateralis 142
Heptagenia sulphurea 73
Hydrometra species 42
Hydropsyche contubernalis 158
Isoperla grammatica 160
Leptophlebia marginata 78
Leptophlebia vespertina 78
Leuctra fusca 188
Leuctra geniculata 188
Libellula depressa 39
Limnephilus lunatus 152
Limnaea peregna 199
Mystacides longicornis 159
Nepa species 43
Notonecta species 42
Paraleptophlebia cincta 144
Paraleptophlebia submarginata 84
Perlodes microcephala 98
Philopotamus montanus 94
Phoxinus phoxinus 204
Phrygania grandis 154
Phrygania striata 154
Phyllopertha horticola 174
Potamophylax latipennis 150
Procloëon bifidum 122
Pyrrhosoma nymphula 175
Rana temporaria 110
Ranatra species 43
Rhyacophila dorsalis 187
Rithrogena germanica 66
Rithrogena semicolorata 70
Sericostoma personatum 149
Sialis fuliginosa 108
Sialis lutaria 108
Silo nigricornis 95
Simulium species 170
Siphlonurus lacustris 148
Sympetrum striolatum 38
Taenyopteryx nebulosa 96
Tettigoniidae 171
Tipula maxima 190